SCHOLASTIC
ATLAS OF
EXPLORATION

DINAH STARKEY

Scholastic
Reference

New York   Toronto   London   Auckland   Sydney

CONTENTS

INTRODUCTION

Throughout the world's history, there have always been people who dared to explore places far from where they lived. Often, they had no maps to guide

them and no idea what they would see or whom they would meet. When they returned, they might bring back stories or draw a picture of what they had seen. Later, they kept diaries and drew maps.

Because of their early journeys, people around the world became aware of each other's lives. Eventually, people were able to draw accurate maps of the land areas of Earth.

Today, we still admire the bravery of early

explorers, but we also know they often acted cruelly. In their ignorance, they sometimes destroyed the people, cultures, and places they "discovered."

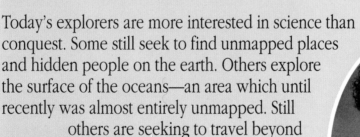

Today's explorers are more interested in science than conquest. Some still seek to find unmapped places and hidden people on the earth. Others explore the surface of the oceans—an area which until recently was almost entirely unmapped. Still

others are seeking to travel beyond the planet into the solar system and beyond. All the explorers in this book are men, but many of today's and tomorrow's explorers are women, too.

HOW THE MAPS WORK

Most of the pages in this book feature a large map showing the routes taken by the explorers. On each of these maps you will find:

A compass to show the direction taken by the explorers and the relation of one place to another

A scale to show the distances covered by the explorers and the relative distance between one place and another

```
0   100   200   400 m
```

A key to the map to show the routes taken by individual explorers. Where an explorer has made more than one journey, the dates of his different journeys are given.

```
KEY TO MAP
~~~~~   Park 1795~96
- - -   Park 1805~6
.......  Caillié
```

Sometimes you will see that a place has been given two names. For example:

Molucca Islands
(Spice Islands)

This occurs when a place that is now known by the first name shown (Molucca Islands) was known at the point of history in question by the second name shown (Spice Islands).

Sometimes you will see that a place has been given only a name in brackets. For example:

(Babylon)

This happens when a place existed at the point of history in question, but now no longer exists.

4

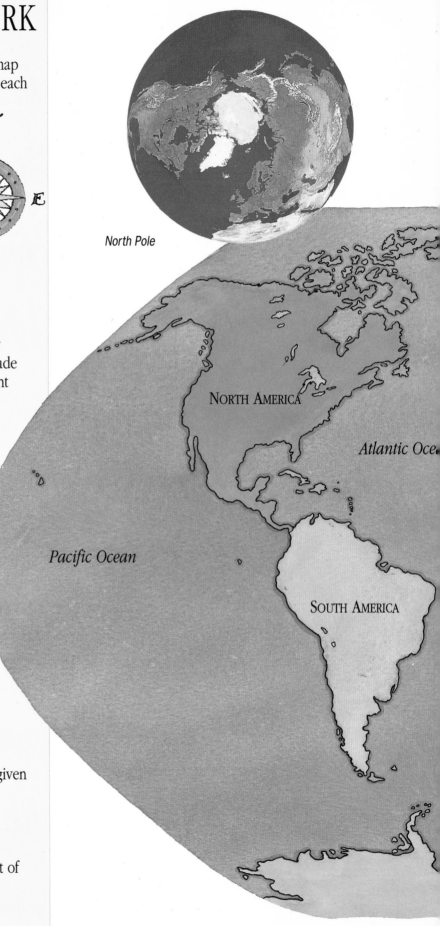

North Pole

NORTH AMERICA

Atlantic Oce

Pacific Ocean

SOUTH AMERICA

WORLD MAP

Below is a map showing the continents and oceans of the world. This is for your reference when following the explorers' routes described in this book. The maps with the explorers' routes show only the part of the world that the explorers traveled. By referring to this world map, you can see the relative distance covered by the explorers and the location of their journeys.

It should be noted that different map projections are used throughout the book, depending on the area being illustrated. For example, a map of the Antarctic, such as the one found on pages 54-55, shows the area of the Antarctic as seen from above. (See also the aerial view of the South Pole on this page.) Both are accurate views of Antarctica. However, when the Antarctic is shown using a different projection, as it is in the world map on this page, you can see that it appears quite different, both in its shape and area.

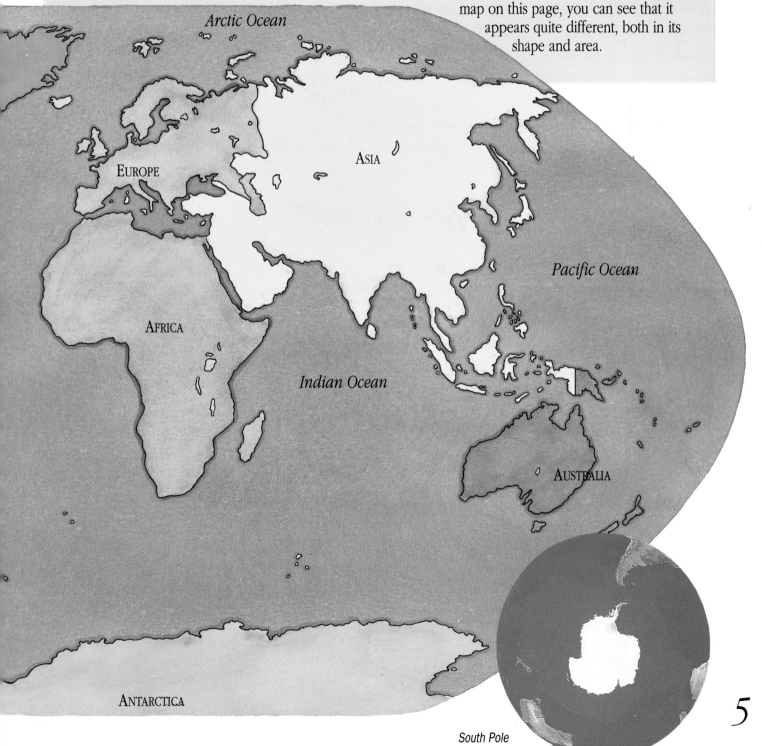

Arctic Ocean

ASIA

EUROPE

Pacific Ocean

AFRICA

Indian Ocean

AUSTRALIA

ANTARCTICA

South Pole

THE EXPLORERS OF THE ANCIENT WORLD

THE EGYPTIANS

Who was the first person to go exploring? We don't know. We do know, however, the first explorer to be named: he was called Harkhuf and he lived in Egypt.

Over 4,000 years ago, the king of Egypt sent Harkhuf into Africa to look for rare woods and treasure. He traveled overland, taking with him a great train of camels and donkeys, known together as a "caravan." It took Harkhuf's caravan several months to reach the area now known as the Sudan, in the north of Africa.

Harkhuf brought back ivory, ebony, and fur, as well as a gifted dancer, who may have been a member of one of the African Pygmy tribes.

Nearly 800 years later, Queen Hatshepsut of Egypt sent sailors to the Land of Punt, which was probably in modern-day Sudan or Somalia. The Egyptians took presents for the king and queen of Punt. When they returned to Egypt, their ships were laden with cinnamon wood and ebony, gold and ivory, monkeys, panther skins, and 31 young frankincense trees, each one in its own pot.

FRANKINCENSE TREES

When burning, the resin of the frankincense tree gives off a sweet smell. The Egyptians did this in their temples to please the gods.

England

MEDITERRANEAN

AFRICA

KEY TO MAP
- ······· Harkhuf
- ——— Hatshepsut
- – – – Phoenician voyages

0   100   200   400 m

KEY DATES (BC means Before Christ)	
● **2270 BC** Harkhuf's expedition set out	● **1493 BC** Queen Hatshepsut sent her expedition to Punt
● **1700–1450 BC** Minoan civilization at its height	● **1100–300 BC** Phoenicians traded throughout the Mediterranean region

AFTER THE EGYPTIANS

THE BABYLONIANS

In southwest Asia the Babylonians studied the sky and tried to solve the mystery of what was beyond the Earth. They decided that the Earth was round and that it was encircled by seas. They thought there were islands in the seas, which made stepping stones to heaven. The Babylonians were the first people to name the four points of the compass.

THE MINOANS

The Minoans of Crete traded throughout the Mediterranean. They made pottery decorated with spirals and sea creatures. People are still finding bits of it today.

THE PHOENICIANS

The Phoenicians lived in northwest Syria. They were brilliant sailors, trading in cedar wood, glass, and Tyrian purple dye.

On a mission for King Solomon, the Phoenicians sailed to a place called Ophir, which was probably situated somewhere on the southwest coast of Arabia. They brought back gold and silver, apes and peacocks, ivory, and cedar wood.

They sailed all over the Mediterranean, down the coast of Africa and further. Some people think they came all the way to England to buy tin, but we can't be sure because the Phoenicians never wrote anything down. They kept their routes secret for fear other people would use them. The routes are still unknown.

BLACK SEA

ASIA

Syria

Crete

(Byblos)

Tyre

(Babylon)

Egypt

The Sudan

Nile

RED SEA

(Arabia)

BABYLONIAN MAP

This is one of the oldest maps of the world. It was made in Babylon in the 7th century BC.

(The Land of Punt)

7

THE GREEKS

The people of ancient Greece lived about 2,000 years later than the Egyptians and Babylonians. They were interested in all kinds of learning. The first true scientists were Greeks.

In the 4th century BC, a Greek named Aristotle proved that the world was round. He noticed that the line where the sky met the Earth (the horizon) was very slightly curved. He showed that it was curved because the world was round.

It was the ancient Greeks who made the first proper maps. Egyptian and Babylonian maps were not very accurate. The people who drew them invented the parts they didn't know because they didn't believe that accuracy mattered. But the Greeks tried hard to find out more about the world so that they could draw better maps. When a sailor returned from foreign lands, he would tell the mapmakers about everything he had seen and they would draw it carefully. If they couldn't find out any information about an area, they left it blank to show that they knew nothing about it. They didn't make anything up.

Greek maps were better than any that had existed in the world before. They were also better than many that came later. In fact, they were so good that when Columbus set off to look for the Indies in 1492, he took with him a copy of a Greek map that was more than 1,000 years old. After all that time, it was still the best map he could find. It was called the Ptolemy map because it had been drawn by a Greek named Ptolemy.

LATITUDE AND LONGITUDE

The Greeks invented new ways of showing the world clearly. A Greek called Eratosthenes was the first to draw lines of latitude and longitude on a map. These are imaginary lines, still used by mapmakers to divide up the world. Lines of latitude go across the world; lines of longitude go from top to bottom. The equator is a line of latitude.

ALEXANDER THE GREAT

In 334 BC Alexander the Great, the king of Greece, took a whole army exploring. He planned to conquer the neighboring empire of Persia. He led his army into Egypt, where he founded a city, which he named Alexandria. He traveled further and further to the east over the huge mountains of the Hindu Kush until his army reached the wide Indus River. Alexander ordered his men to build a bridge of boats, and in this way they crossed the river.

Alexander wanted to advance further east, but his men were tired of traveling and they refused to go any further. With his army, Alexander sailed down the Indus River to find out where it led, aiming to return to Greece by sea. The men reached Susa in the Persian Gulf in 324 BC, but Alexander never got home to Greece. He died, possibly of malaria, at age 32.

PYTHEAS

One of the greatest Greek explorers was Pytheas of Massilia (Marseilles). He sailed along the west coast of France and all the way around Britain. He sailed north of Britain for six days until he came to a land known as Thule. It was a sunless place where people lived on millet, herbs, berries, and fruits. He sailed on until he came to a place where the sea froze over and there were glaciers and volcanoes. We think he may have reached Norway or Iceland, but the book in which he wrote of his journeys has been lost and no one can be certain.

KEY DATES
- **384-322 BC** Aristotle lived
- **334 BC** Alexander led his army from Greece
- ***330 BC** Pytheas sailed from Marseilles to Thule
- ***276-194 BC** Eratosthenes lived
- ***2nd century AD** Ptolemy lived

*exact date unknown

9

THE VIKINGS

The Vikings came from Denmark, Norway, and Sweden. These are countries surrounded by water with little good farming land. The Vikings made their living from the sea: from fishing, piracy, and trading with other countries. They went as far as Russia, trading in amber, furs, and whale oil, and they were always on the lookout for new land where they could settle and farm. They were great explorers.

The Vikings were also excellent sailors and knew how to find their way across the open sea without using landmarks. They used the sun and stars to help them.

When a Norwegian named Floki Vilgerdasson set sail from Norway in 860 AD to look for new land, he took three ravens with him to help him find the way. He knew these birds can sense when land is near. Floki let the first one go; it flew back to Norway. Later, he let the second one go; it flew around, then settled on the ship. But when at last he released the third raven, it flew ahead of the ship. Floki knew the bird must have found land, so he followed it. He soon sighted Iceland.

KEY TO MAP
——— Floki Vilgerdasson
– – – Eric the Red
········ Leif Ericson

Baffin Island

Greenland

NORTH AMERICA (Vinland)

ATLANTIC OCEAN

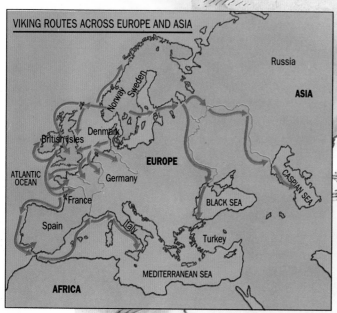

VIKING ROUTES ACROSS EUROPE AND ASIA

Russia

ASIA

Norway   Sweden

British Isles   Denmark

EUROPE

ATLANTIC OCEAN   Germany

CASPIAN SEA

France

BLACK SEA

Spain   Italy   Turkey

MEDITERRANEAN SEA

AFRICA

KEY DATES
● **860** AD Floki Vilgerdasson sailed to Iceland

● **981** AD Eric the Red sailed to Greenland
● **1000** AD Leif Ericson landed in Vinland

10

VIKING SHIPS

When the Vikings went raiding, they used long narrow ships (longships) to creep up rivers and take their enemies by surprise. When they set off to look for new lands, they took a different kind of ship called a *knorr*. This was bigger and broader than a longship and it was clinker-built. This means that the planks overlapped, which stopped water from leaking in and made the ships stronger. Knorrs were well-built enough to stand up to the fierce weather of the Atlantic and they could hold a lot. Viking explorers took women servants with them. Packed into the same boat were also cattle, pigs, sheep, and seeds. Knorrs were not covered over and these long journeys were cold, miserable, and dangerous.

VIKING SAGAS

The Vikings liked to make up long tales about their brave deeds. These tales are called sagas and some of them tell of the adventures of the Viking explorers. These men were great boasters, so we can't be sure that the sagas were absolutely true. We can still learn from them, however. One saga tells of an adventurer named Eric the Red. He lived in Iceland, but he had to leave in a hurry because he had killed someone. He left for three years, and in 981 AD he went sailing to look for a new land. He found a country that seemed rich and fertile. The sea was full of fish. He called this new country Greenland and settled there with his family. Eric had a son called Leif. The Viking stories call him Leif the Lucky because, they say, he found a new land. He was sailing near Greenland in the year 1000 AD when his ship ran into storms. It was swept westward until Leif and his crew landed on a strange shore. They found fields of wild wheat and grapevines, so they called the new country Vinland. Scholars think Vinland was Newfoundland.

Another story says that a trader named Bjarni Herjulfsson was the first person to sight America. Whatever the truth of these sagas, it seems likely that the Vikings did reach the American continent long before Columbus.

Left: Eric the Red in Greenland

11

THE MIDDLE AGES

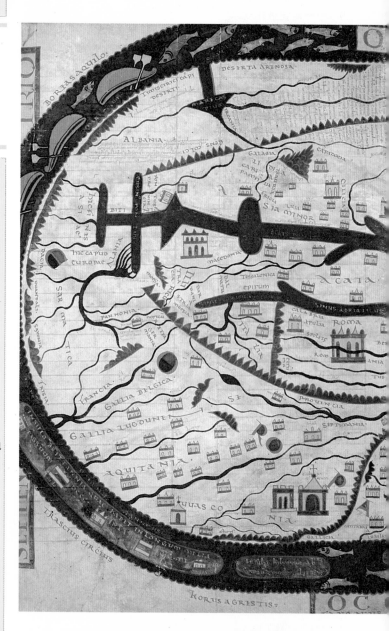

The map shown here was made 900 years ago. By this time, the fine maps of the ancient Greeks had been lost. Most people believed that the world was flat and that if you sailed too far away from land, you would meet terrible monsters, darkness, and danger.

Europeans thought Africa was a land of mystery. They had heard tales about dog-headed men, cannibals, and magical fountains. Somewhere far inland, they believed, was a kingdom that was Christian, with a king named Prester John. People also believed in a river of gold and thought travelers on it might find the Garden of Eden, surrounded by a wall of fire.

People of the Middle Ages had forgotten the skills of earlier times. No longer did sailors dare to cross the open sea. Their ships were not as easy to handle as the Viking boats. Travel was a slow and dangerous business. Most people stayed at home.

Those in Europe who did travel were the traders, who crossed the countries of Europe; pilgrims, who made their way to Spain and Jerusalem; and knights, who went on crusades to the Holy Land to fight the Arabs who had taken Jerusalem. Here they had their first taste of the many spices from Asia.

GENGHIS KHAN

In 1206 a new emperor was crowned. He was Genghis Khan, ruler of the Mongols. These people were nomads who traveled the great plain of Mongolia, a vast region of central Asia, with their herds of cattle. They were fine horsemen and fierce fighters. Genghis Khan built up a huge army that swept through Asia, capturing enormous areas of land. By 1215, they had reached Beijing in China. When the Khan died, the Mongol Empire stretched from the Yellow Sea to the Caspian Sea. His sons and grandsons went on to invade Russia, Poland, and Hungary.

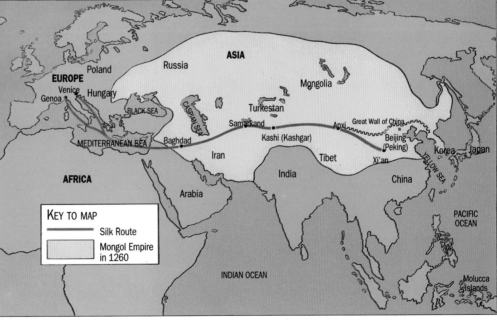

VENICE AND GENOA

Venice and Genoa (far left on map), at the end of the Silk Route, were busy ports. Ships brought rich goods from Asia to Italy, France, England and Spain. As a result, the cities became very wealthy – Venice was Europe's richest city in the 13th century.

THE SILK ROUTE

The Silk Route consisted of several different roads leading from China, where silk was first made over 4,500 years ago, to the Middle East (in the western part of Asia) and Europe. Merchants used it for trading goods such as silk, porcelain, gold, and ivory.

MARCO POLO

It was 1298. Two men were in prison. To pass the time, one started telling the other tales of his life. He told of elephants and jewels, magicians and fire-eaters, and of a land rich and powerful beyond imagination. The prisoner's name was Marco Polo, and he was describing his 17 years in China at the court of the great Kublai Khan (grandson of Genghis Khan).

Marco Polo was born in Venice in 1254. At the age of about 17, he set out with his father and uncle along the Silk Route to the Mongolian capital of Shang-tu. The journey, which lasted more than three years, took them over huge mountains and across wide deserts to the great Khan's summer palace at Shang-tu. Polo became a servant of the Khan. He traveled all over the Mongol Empire, taking note of everything he saw. On his return, he was captured by the Genoese, who were at war with the people of Venice. His fellow prisoner, Rustichello, wrote down Polo's stories in a book known as *The Book of Marvels*.

THE IMPORTANCE OF MARCO POLO

Marco Polo told of gold, silver, diamonds, rubies, and pearls. He described the spices that grew in Java: nutmeg, cloves, peppers and many others. He made Kublai Khan's empire sound like a treasure house.

People began to think seriously about ways of getting to Asia because they believed that, once there, they could make their fortune. Christopher Columbus was one of the explorers who read Marco Polo's book and dreamed of finding a way to Java and the Spice Islands.

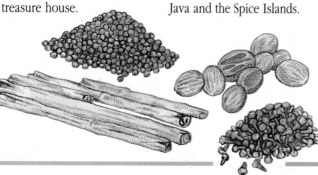

KUBLAI KHAN'S EMPIRE

According to Marco Polo's book, the walls of the Khan's palace were covered with silver and gold. The palace glittered from afar like a crystal.

In the winter Kublai Khan and his court went hunting. The Khan rode on an elephant in a pavilion covered with lion skins and gold cloth. He hunted with hawks and leopards. Huge numbers of animals were killed on these hunts.

IBN BATTUTA

Ibn Battuta was born in Morocco in 1304. He was on a pilgrimage to Mecca when he had a dream. He dreamed that he was riding on the back of a great bird that carried him far away into the East. He believed this meant that he must travel east as far as he could. So began a life of journeying from North Africa to China, in which Ibn Battuta encountered thieves and shipwreck, plagues, and storms. Sometimes he was greeted by kings and showered with gifts. Once he was captured by bandits and threatened with death. Of all the Muslim travelers, Ibn Battuta was the greatest.

TRAVELING IN THE KHAN'S EMPIRE

The Khan gave orders for good roads to be built throughout his empire. Many trees were planted along the roads to provide shade in the summer. The Khan's messengers, who were chosen for their swiftness, traveled these roads with bells hanging from them so that everyone could hear them coming.

The most important of the Khan's servants carried a gold tablet. This was a sign to show people that the Khan's servants could go wherever they pleased and that people had to supply them with fresh horses, food, shelter, and any other help they needed. Marco Polo, his father, and his uncle carried one of these gold tablets with them whenever they traveled.

KEY TO MAP
— Marco Polo
----- Ibn Battuta

ASIA

Mongolia
Gobi Desert

Shang-tu

Beijing

Kashgar

China

Baghdad

Himalayas

(Arabia)

Mecca

India

PACIFIC OCEAN

INDIAN OCEAN

Java

Molucca Islands
(Spice Islands)

EUROPEANS IN ASIAN LANDS

Ever since the time of the Crusades in the Middle Ages, rich people in Europe had been buying silks and spices from Asia. They were willing to pay high prices for these items. Traders knew that as long as they could travel between Europe and Asia, they could run a profitable business. By the 15th century, though, parts of the Silk Route had been blocked off. The route ran through Turkey and Arabia, and the people who lived here were Muslims, and enemies to all Christians. They barred the road and fought off any Christian trader who tried to pass.

By 1450 European sailors had learned how to use a compass to steer a course. They no longer needed to stay close to the coast all the time. Ships were improving; they were becoming faster and easier to handle. Some ships used the lateen sail, which enabled them to sail against the wind by zigzagging ("beating"). This is also known as "sailing close to the wind."

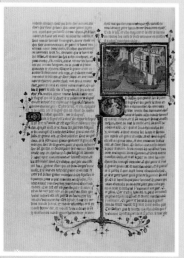

Marco Polo's book told people about the riches of Asia. Then, in 1410, another important book appeared: Ptolemy's *Guide to Geography*. This book had been lost and forgotten for 1,300 years in Europe. Now a copy was found and translated. The overland route to Asia was blocked, but Ptolemy's map showed that it might be possible to find a sea route to the Spice Islands via Africa. The great age of exploration had begun.

LATEEN SAILS

Early ships used square sails. They only worked well with the wind right behind them. But the lateen sail was triangular and, if needed, it could be set to catch a less favorable wind.

JUNKS

Cheng Ho's ships were called junks. They were enormous, some carrying as many as five sails. The Chinese still use junks today.

CHENG HO

While the merchants of Europe were looking for a sea route to India and the Far East, the admiral Cheng Ho set out from China to travel west. He took with him a huge fleet that included 62 treasure ships and 250 smaller vessels. He made seven journeys across the China Sea and the Indian Ocean, visiting 30 countries and gathering information about them. His fleet carried up to 30,000 people, including doctors, translators, merchants, crafts-

people, and priests. The ships stayed at sea for months at a time. On his seventh voyage, Cheng Ho's ships sailed a distance of over 12,600 miles.

The Chinese knew more about keeping healthy at sea than the Europeans did. Cheng Ho's crew grew vegetables on board, and doctors looked after the sick. Nevertheless, the journeys were full of hazards and many people did not survive them.

0 200 400 600 m

ASIA

Mongolia

Gobi Desert

China

Loyang

Japan

(Persia)

Tibet

Himalayas

Yangtze

Hormuz

Ganges

Chittagong

India

Philippine Islands

SOUTH CHINA SEA

Calicut

Maldive Islands

INDIAN OCEAN

Borneo

Sumatra

Molucca Islands (Spice Islands)

Java

KEY TO MAP
- - - Main Silk Route
– · – Main Spice Route
—— Cheng Ho

17

VASCO DA GAMA

Vasco da Gama was a Portuguese explorer born around 1460. This was the year of the death of Prince Henry of Portugal (below), who was also known as

Henry the Navigator because of his interest in exploration.

In 1433 Prince Henry sent a ship from Portugal to sail down the west coast of Africa as far as possible, then come back and report on what had been discovered. It was all part of his drive to find a sea route to the Spice Islands.

For 15 years he had been gathering together map-makers, sea captains, geographers, shipbuilders, and every kind of expert he could think of to help him in the project. To persuade them, he offered them land and gold. While the experts thought up new ship designs and ways of navigating, Prince Henry's sea captains put them into practice.

The first ships didn't go very far. Sailors believed that beyond Cape Bojador lay the Sea of Darkness, and they were afraid to go on. The ship sent by Prince Henry in 1433 was the first to get past Cape Bojador. Despite Henry's death, the Portuguese continued their voyages of exploration. By 1497 Portuguese ships had reached the southernmost tip of Africa. Under Vasco da Gama, the greatest of the Portuguese voyages was about to begin.

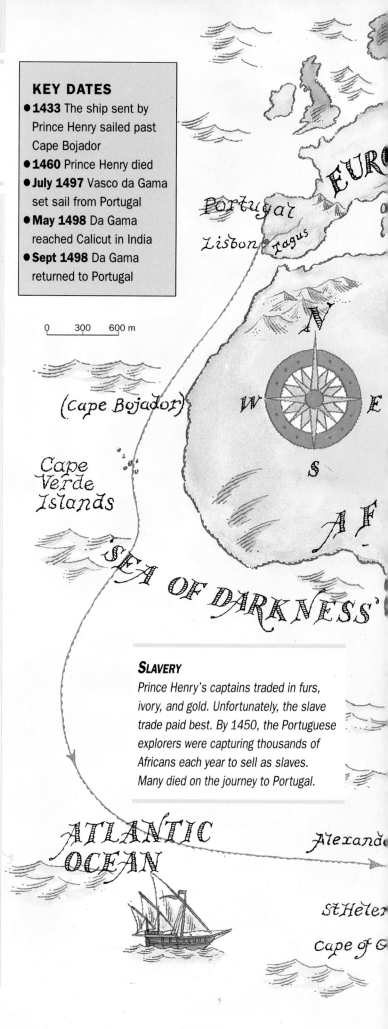

KEY DATES
- **1433** The ship sent by Prince Henry sailed past Cape Bojador
- **1460** Prince Henry died
- **July 1497** Vasco da Gama set sail from Portugal
- **May 1498** Da Gama reached Calicut in India
- **Sept 1498** Da Gama returned to Portugal

0   300   600 m

SLAVERY
Prince Henry's captains traded in furs, ivory, and gold. Unfortunately, the slave trade paid best. By 1450, the Portuguese explorers were capturing thousands of Africans each year to sell as slaves. Many died on the journey to Portugal.

THE JOURNEY

On July 8, 1497, Vasco da Gama set sail from the Tagus River in Portugal. He steered toward the Cape Verde Islands and then straight out to sea in a wide sweep that took the crew far out of sight of land for two months. At last, on November 7, they sighted St. Helena Bay. The crew ran up flags, fired off guns, and dressed in their best to celebrate.

It took two more months to round the Cape of Good Hope and sail up the coast of East Africa. On January 25, da Gama had his first glimpse of the great Arab *dhows* sailing across the Indian Ocean. They were heavy with gold, silver, cloves, peppers, ginger, pearls and rubies.

At Malindi, da Gama picked up an Indian pilot, Ibn Majid, to help them steer the correct course, and on May 20, they reached the Indian port of Calicut. Calicut was a very rich port; the Arabs who traded there brought fine silks with them and gave its ruler, the samorin, wonderful presents. Da Gama had few gifts to offer and what he had didn't please the samorin. The people of Calicut didn't want to trade with the Portuguese. Da Gama managed to buy some pepper and cinnamon and soon set off for home. The travelers had a hard journey with bad weather all the way. They landed in Portugal in September to a hero's welcome: Vasco da Gama had found the sea route to India.

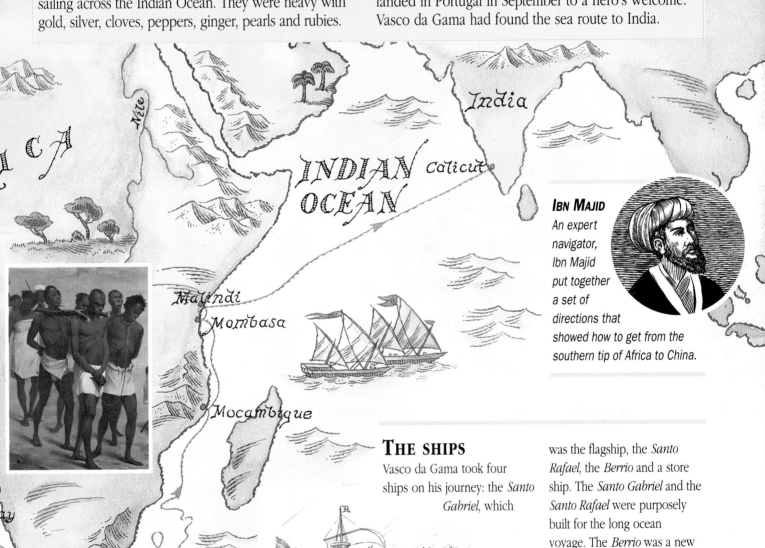

IBN MAJID
An expert navigator, Ibn Majid put together a set of directions that showed how to get from the southern tip of Africa to China.

THE SHIPS
Vasco da Gama took four ships on his journey: the *Santo Gabriel*, which was the flagship, the *Santo Rafael*, the *Berrio* and a store ship. The *Santo Gabriel* and the *Santo Rafael* were purposely built for the long ocean voyage. The *Berrio* was a new *caravel* – a tall, fast ship with lateen sails for sailing against the wind. On board the ships were 170 men and enough supplies for three years.

CHRISTOPHER COLUMBUS

The port of Genoa in Italy was an exciting place for adventurers in the late 15th century. In the harbor sailors from as far away as Africa and Iceland swapped stories of the sea. A young Genoese boy named Christopher Columbus listened. The stories made him want to sail the oceans, and his seafaring adventures began at the age of 14. These journeys, and conversations with his mapmaker brother, gave Columbus the idea for a grand voyage. He believed he could reach Asia by going west across the Atlantic Ocean. Columbus hoped to bring back precious silks and spices by sailing on this new route.

Such a daring expedition was very costly, and it was years before Columbus found someone who would pay for the trip. Eventually, though, King Ferdinand and Queen Isabella of Spain agreed to provide the ships, sailors, and supplies that Columbus needed. In 1492 Columbus was able to set sail from the Spanish port of Palos.

THE NORTH ATLANTIC WINDS

Columbus was able to cross the North Atlantic because he understood the ocean's winds. In the north, the winds blow from west to east, but further south, they blow the opposite way, from east to west. Columbus kept to the south on his outward journey and returned to Spain by a northern route.

LANDFALL

On October 12, 1492, after sailing for 33 days, the ships arrived at a small island in the Bahamas. We cannot be sure exactly which island it was, although scholars think it was San Salvador. The people living on the island called it Guanahaní. The islanders were curious and friendly. They came out in canoes to meet the ships. Columbus and the sailors went ashore carrying the Spanish banner and the admiral's flag, and they claimed the island for Spain.

THE NATIVE PEOPLES

The Arawak people living on the islands Columbus reached were generous and peace-loving. They were happy to share their food and

possessions with the strangers who arrived at their shore. However, the sailors became greedy. They seized cotton, cinnamon, and precious stones. Later, they took prisoners from among the islanders to sell as slaves.

The Arawaks caught diseases such as smallpox from the Spaniards, which killed them in large numbers. Fifty years after Columbus' expedition first set sail, Hispaniola's native population of about 250,000 had all died out.

0   200   400   600 m

Azores   Lisbon

EUROPE

Genoa

Italy

Portugal   Spain

Palos

Canary Islands

Cape Verde Islands

ATLANTIC OCEAN

AFRICA

Explorers' Supplies

Columbus' three ships carried enough supplies for a year. They took:

BARRELS OF FRESH WATER

JARS OF OIL

SALT

FLOUR

SALTED MEATS

NETS

HOOKS AND FISHING LINES

WOOD FOR FUEL

SACKING TO SLEEP ON

BEADS AND RED WOOLEN CAPS FOR TRADING

ROUTE TO THE INDIES?

Columbus wanted to be the first person to find a western sea route from Europe to the Indies (the name given to Southeast Asia, India and Indochina). Like other Europeans at that time, he did not know that North and

ASIA — NORTH AMERICA — EUROPE — The Indies — ATLANTIC OCEAN — AFRICA — PACIFIC OCEAN — SOUTH AMERICA — AUSTRALIA

South America lay in the way. When he landed on one of the islands in the Bahamas, he was sure that he had in fact

reached somewhere in the Indies. It wasn't until much later that Columbus discovered his mistake. This is why he called the inhabitants of the island "Indians," and why the islands off the east coast of America are known today as the West Indies.

21

MORE ON NEXT PAGE

LIFE ON BOARD

The sailors on board Columbus' ships spent much of their time, both night and day, up in the rigging, adjusting the sails to make the ships travel as fast as possible.

They cooked their food on deck in large pots heated by a wood fire. Only one hot meal was served each day, and that was at 11 o'clock, when the men on watch came off duty to be replaced by a new group of men.

The crew squatted on deck to eat, drinking broth from bowls and picking out the meat and fish with their fingers. They also ate hard bread with their meals. When not working, sailors sometimes fished from the ship's deck. Fresh fish for lunch was considered a treat.

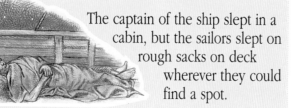

The captain of the ship slept in a cabin, but the sailors slept on rough sacks on deck wherever they could find a spot.

THE SANTA MARIA

Columbus was captain of the *Santa Maria*, the biggest of the ships. It crossed the Atlantic from the Canary Islands in a little more than a month. This was a fast crossing, and the crew arrived in the Bahamas not only alive but fit and well. Modern replicas (working copies) of the ship have never been as fast as the *Santa Maria*.

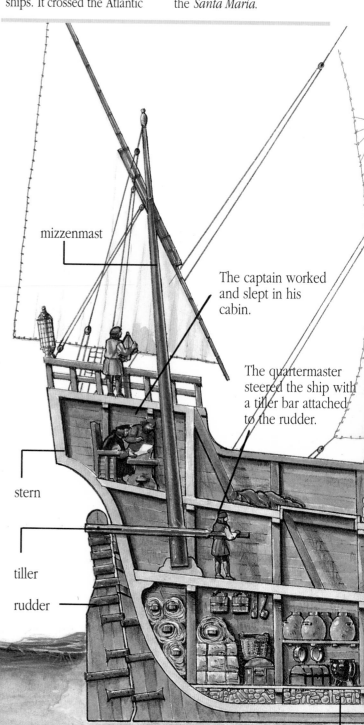

mizzenmast

The captain worked and slept in his cabin.

The quartermaster steered the ship with a tiller bar attached to the rudder.

stern

tiller

rudder

Ballast was used to keep the ship stable.

THE SHIPS

Columbus took three ships on his journey west: the *Niña*, the *Pinta*, and the *Santa Maria*.

All three ships were caravels—tall-sided sailing ships with three masts that first appeared in the 15th century. The *Niña* was fast and agile with triangular (or lateen) sails, good for sailing against the wind; the *Pinta* was larger and square-sailed. These sails were better for sailing with the wind.

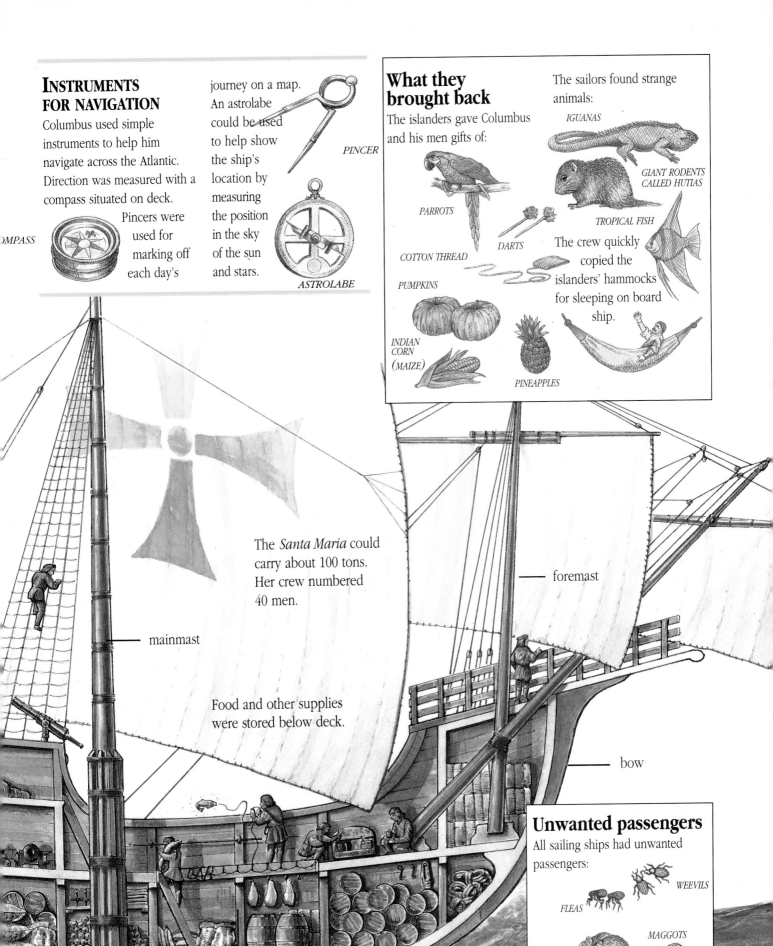

INSTRUMENTS FOR NAVIGATION

Columbus used simple instruments to help him navigate across the Atlantic. Direction was measured with a compass situated on deck.

COMPASS

Pincers were used for marking off each day's journey on a map. An astrolabe could be used to help show the ship's location by measuring the position in the sky of the sun and stars.

PINCER

ASTROLABE

What they brought back

The islanders gave Columbus and his men gifts of:

The sailors found strange animals:

IGUANAS

PARROTS

GIANT RODENTS CALLED HUTIAS

COTTON THREAD

DARTS

TROPICAL FISH

The crew quickly copied the islanders' hammocks for sleeping on board ship.

PUMPKINS

INDIAN CORN (MAIZE)

PINEAPPLES

The *Santa Maria* could carry about 100 tons. Her crew numbered 40 men.

foremast

mainmast

Food and other supplies were stored below deck.

bow

Unwanted passengers

All sailing ships had unwanted passengers:

WEEVILS

FLEAS

MAGGOTS

RATS

hold

23

FERDINAND MAGELLAN

Ferdinand Magellan, born in about 1480 in Portugal, had the same idea as Christopher Columbus. He too believed that he could get to the Spice Islands by sailing west from Europe. Columbus had found that

America lay in the way, but Magellan thought he could find a sea passage through America.

Magellan needed a sponsor to pay for the voyage. He was Portuguese, but the Portuguese king had treated him badly, so Magellan offered his plan to Charles V, king of Spain.

THE CREW

Spanish sailors didn't want to serve with Magellan because he was Portuguese. Magellan had to take anyone who would sign on, whether the person was a skilled seaman or not. Some of the crew were prisoners, released from jail in return for sailing with Magellan.

THE SHIPS

Charles V gave Magellan five ships: the Trinidad, the San Antonio, the Concepcion, the Victoria, and the Santiago. The boats were small, old, and patched up—not fit for a long journey in rough seas. Magellan accepted them because they were the best he could get.

KEY DATES
- **Sept 1519** Magellan's fleet left Seville in Spain
- **Nov 1519** The ships reached the coast of Brazil
- **Mar 1520** The fleet reached Patagonia
- **Oct 1520** The Magellan Strait was discovered
- **Nov 1520** The ships emerged into the South Pacific
- **Mar 1521** The ships reached Guam
- **Apr 1521** Magellan was killed in the Philippines
- **Sept 1522** The Victoria returned to Spain

24

THE JOURNEY

In September 1519 Magellan and his men said their prayers and set off from southern Spain. At first, all went well. The small fleet reached South America and stocked up with fresh food. Then they sailed down the coast of South America, looking for a passage through to the Pacific, but they couldn't find a strait (a strip of water) to let them pass. They had to sail further and further south towards the South Pole. The weather was becoming colder, and they were running out of food.

The crew revolted against the leaders. Magellan hanged the instigators and continued the search. At last, in October 1520, they found a strait. Magellan named it after himself—the Magellan Strait. You can still see it on today's maps. It took 38 days to sail through to the Pacific, then they found themselves sailing for

weeks on end with no sign of land. The drinking water was stinking and slimy and the crew had to eat rats. One of the captains deserted and sailed his ship, the *San Antonio*, back to Spain.

In March they landed at Guam. Then the ships headed for the Moluccas, the Spice Islands, but Magellan never got there. He was caught in a war in the Philippines and died with a spear through his heart.

Magellan's ship was burned, and now only three ships remained. One was left behind. The other two reached the Molucca Islands and loaded a rich cargo of spices to take back to Spain. One of these ships was taken captive. Only the *Victoria* reached home. This was the first ship to have sailed around the world.

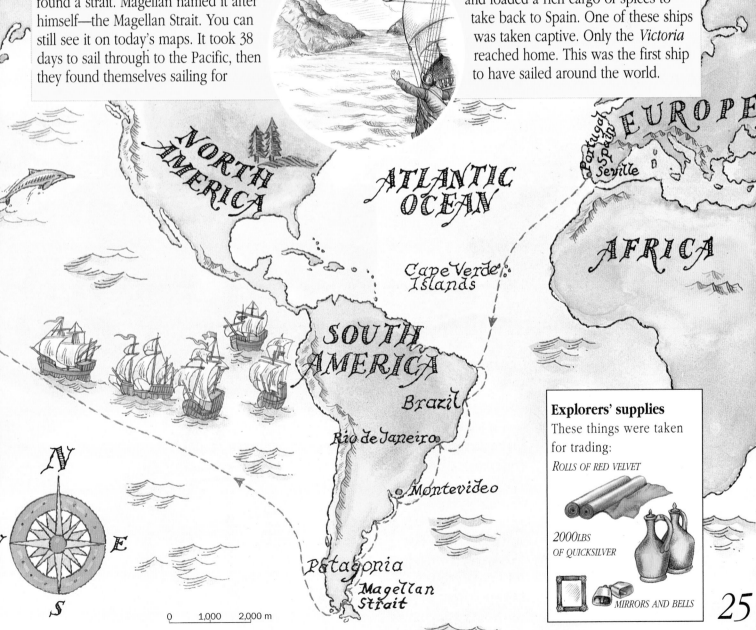

NORTH AMERICA

ATLANTIC OCEAN

EUROPE

Portugal Spain
Seville

AFRICA

Cape Verde Islands

SOUTH AMERICA

Brazil

Rio de Janeiro

Montevideo

Patagonia

Magellan Strait

N
W E
S

0   1,000   2,000 m

Explorers' supplies
These things were taken for trading:

ROLLS OF RED VELVET

2000LBS OF QUICKSILVER

MIRRORS AND BELLS

25

MORE ON NEXT PAGE

MUTINY ON BOARD

Life was hard on board ship. Sailors spent all their time on deck, working, sleeping, and eating there. Towards the end of a long journey, food became very scarce. On Magellan's voyage the crew had to eat rotten biscuits, ox hides and even rats and sawdust. Anyone who fell asleep on watch was whipped or dunked in the sea.

The men who sailed on these difficult journeys were often afraid. They believed that they might come to the end of the Earth or that they might sail on and on until they ran out of food and water. Sometimes, when they had traveled for many days without sighting land, they made plans to kill the captain and turn back. This was called mutiny; it was the worst crime of all on board ship. The penalty was death.

The captains of the *Concepcion* and the *Victoria* mutinied against Magellan. They were hanged, drawn, and quartered. Only one man who had joined in the mutiny wasn't killed, because he was a representative of the king. Instead, he was marooned (left behind) on a desert island.

SCURVY

Food was a problem at sea because it could not be kept fresh. At the beginning of a journey, a ship carried fresh fruits and vegetables, but these had to be eaten before they spoiled. Sometimes the men were at sea for months at a time with no fresh food, so they had no vitamin C in their diet. This lack often caused a terrible disease called scurvy. First, the sailors' gums became sore; then they began to bleed and turn black. The men with scurvy couldn't chew their food because their teeth hurt. Soon their teeth fell out. The first thing a captain did when his ship anchored was to send ashore for fresh vegetables and fruits to give to the poor seamen.

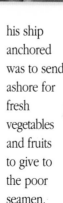

PEOPLE THEY MET

Traveling down the coast of Patagonia, the southernmost part of South America, Magellan's crew met an enormous man who was dancing and singing all alone. He was so tall that their heads hardly reached his waist. He wore big shoes made of skin. Magellan wrote about this in his journal.

When Magellan's ships reached Guam, near the Philippines, the islanders welcomed them. They brought coconut and fruit to trade for iron. Their intention was to be friendly, but Magellan somehow thought they were stealing. He ordered his men to open fire and several of the islanders were killed.

WHAT HAPPENED TO THE SHIPS

The *Santiago* was lost in a storm off Patagonia; the *San Antonio* returned to Spain, taking most of the supplies with her. The *Concepcion* was burned by the crew after Magellan died, as there were not enough men left alive to sail her home. The *Trinidad* was taken captive by the Portuguese, who had taken possession of the Spice Islands. The *Victoria* was the only ship to make it safely home to Spain.

Out of five ships, one returned. Out of 250 men, 18 came back.

HERNANDO CORTES AND THE AZTECS

The Aztec empire stretched over an area of Central America that today belongs to Mexico. The emperor Montezuma ruled from the capital of Tenochtitlán, which is now Mexico City. He lived in a palace and was considered so holy that he never put his feet on the ground— he was carried everywhere.

In the cities, the Aztecs held big markets that sold maize (corn), beans, jewels, weapons, cloaks made of feathers, and little hairless dogs, which the Aztecs ate. There were peppers, tomatoes, and avocados for sale. You could buy cocoa beans to make into chocolate, but this was so expensive that it was kept for special occasions.

THE AZTEC GODS

The Aztecs believed in many different gods. Tláloc, the god of rain, was probably the oldest god. His sister or wife was the goddess of running water. She also protected marriage and newborn babies. There were several gods of farming: Centéotl was the god of maize and Chicomecóatl was the goddess of corn. Quetzalcóatl (above) was the

god of the wind and the arts. The war god, Huitzilopochtli, was one of the most important Aztec gods.

AZTECS AND THE SUN GOD

The Aztecs worshipped the sun. They believed that there had once been five suns and that, one by one, they had all died, until there was just one left. It could only be kept alive by offerings of blood.

Every day, Aztec men, women, and children pricked an ear with a cactus spine to make it bleed. They offered the drops of blood to the Sun God.

Aztec priests sacrificed prisoners of war. They cut open their chests and offered their hearts to the Sun God. The Aztecs believed that the sacrificed people did not die, but went up into the sky to live in happiness with the Sun God.

KEY DATES
- **Feb 1519** Cortés landed in North America
- **Nov 1519** His army entered Tenochtitlán
- **July 1520** His army fought their way out of the city
- **May-Aug 1521** Cortés besieged the city

Mexico City (Tenochtitlán)

PACIFIC OCEAN

0   50   100 m

HERNANDO CORTES

Hernando Cortés came from Spain. He was a *conquistador* (an adventurer and conqueror) who went to America to seek his fortune. When he landed in Veracruz in 1519, he burned his boats to show his men there was no turning back and marched to the Aztec capital, Tenochtitlán.

The Aztecs had never seen strangers like these men, whose faces were pale and skin hairy. They rode on monsters (horses) and carried sticks that spat thunder (guns). The Aztecs thought they were gods.

Cortés and his army reached the capital on November 8, 1519. Montezuma sent them presents and allowed them to enter the city. He even gave them rooms in his own palace. As time passed, however, the Aztecs realized their great mistake.

The Spaniards began to attack the Aztec nobles and kill them for their gold. The Aztecs rose up against the Spaniards. Montezuma tried to calm them, but he was stoned by his own people and soon died.

Cortés' army fought their way out of Tenochtitlán over the bodies of the dead. When Cortés returned with more men, he found the Aztecs weakened by hunger and disease. After a four-month siege, the Spaniards took the city. The Aztec empire was at an end.

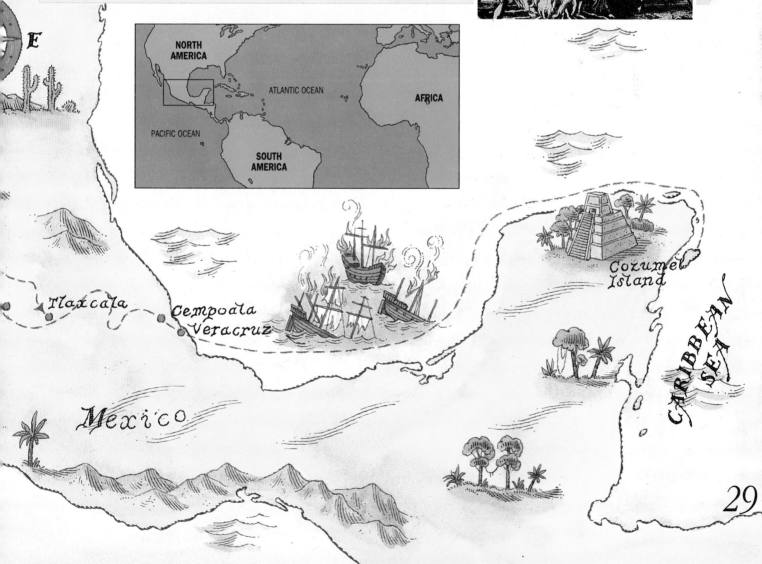

FRANCISCO PIZARRO AND THE INCAS

High up in the Andes, in the country that is now Peru, there was once a great empire. It was ruled by the Inca—an emperor who was worshipped as a god by his people. The people of this empire are known to us as the Incas.

The Inca empire was very rich. It stretched for thousands of miles. The emperor's palace and the Temple of the Sun were in the capital, Cuzco. The Temple was covered with sheets of gold. The Incas believed gold was the sweat of the sun.

The emperor controlled everything. He told his people when to plant and when to harvest, when to make roads and when to go to war.

The Incas built bridges and roads that went over the mountains. The emperor's messengers traveled the roads by foot since they had no animals to carry them. The Incas had

no form of writing, so the runners carried messages in their heads. They also got help from a knotted rope called a *quipu*. Every knot had a special meaning that could be "read."

Orinoco

Colombia

SOUTH AMERICA

Amazon

Brazil

Cuzco

Lake Titicaca

KEY DATES
- **1530** Pizarro landed in Peru
- **Nov 1532** The Spaniards took Atahualpa prisoner
- **Aug 1533** The Spaniards killed Atahualpa

FRANCISCO PIZARRO

Pizarro was a Spanish conquistador. He set out in 1530 for Peru with 180 men and 37 horses to make his fortune. He and his army landed on the west coast of Peru and then began the long climb into the Andes Mountains. They were met by a messenger and guide from Atahualpa, the emperor of the Incas, and led to the hot springs where Atahualpa and his court were relaxing.

Although the Spaniards were greatly outnumbered by the soldiers and courtiers of the emperor, they turned on the astonished Incas with their swords and guns, killing thousands of them. Atahualpa himself was captured by Pizarro.

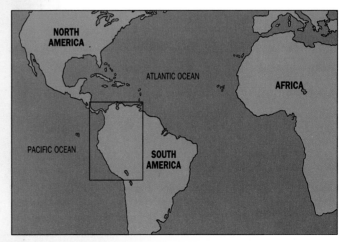

Atahualpa saw that the Spaniards loved gold. He offered to give Pizarro a whole room filled with gold in exchange for his freedom. Pizarro agreed, so Atahualpa sent out word to his people. The Incas stripped their temples to pay the ransom. However, when the room was full, Pizarro broke his promise and had the emperor killed. The Inca empire fell apart and the Spanish became the new rulers of Peru.

EXPLORERS OF NORTH AMERICA

Spain and Portugal had sent out more successful explorers than any other country. Following Vasco da Gama's success in reaching India from Portugal, the Portuguese were able to use the route to the Spice Islands that took them around the southern tip of Africa. The Spanish had shown that there was no easy way to Asia through South America. Other European countries, such as Britain, France, and Holland were eager to send out explorers to new areas. One of these areas was North America, where the land was rich and easy to farm and the waters were full of fish. In the north, there were forests for wood and beavers and deer to hunt for fur; further south were herds of wild buffalo. The main reason, however, for sending explorers to North America was to try to find another route to the Spice Islands.

HENRY HUDSON

Hudson was English, but he worked for the Dutch East India Company, a trading company. The company thought there might be a passage to Asia through North America and it sent Hudson to look.

Hudson made two great journeys. In 1609 he sailed up the east coast of North America looking for a way through to the Pacific. He found the great Hudson River, which is named after him. He did not find a passage.

In 1610 he set out again. This time he was working for the English. He sailed much further north and found a strait (a way through) and a great bay, both of which now bear his name. As winter came on, the Hudson Bay froze over and his ship, the *Discovery*, was trapped. The crew mutinied, and Hudson, his son, and seven sailors were cast adrift. They were never heard from again.

KEY DATES
- **1603-15** Champlain explored Canada
- **1609** Hudson found the Hudson River
- **1610** Hudson discovered Hudson Bay and Hudson Strait
- **1797-1812** Thompson explored the northwest of North America
- **1806** Lewis and Clark reached the Pacific coast of North America

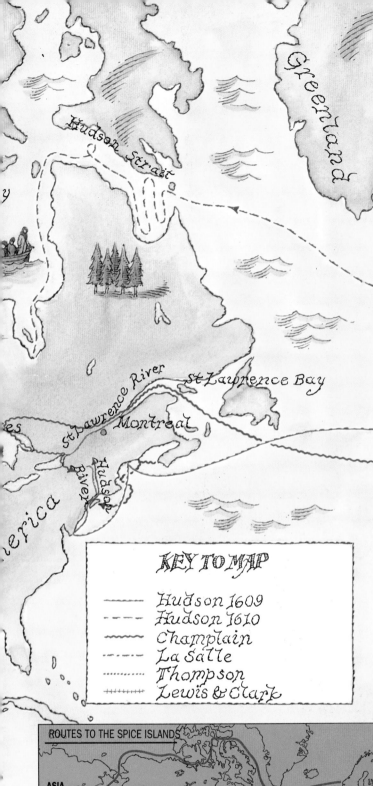

OVERLAND EXPLORERS

The French sent Samuel de Champlain (below) to explore Canada. Between 1603 and 1615, he explored the St. Lawrence River and the Great Lakes. He was guided by Indians and traveled much of the way by canoe. Champlain found the way for the French fur traders who later settled in Canada.

Another Frenchman, Robert Cavelier, Sieur de la Salle, sailed from the Great Lakes down the Mississippi River. In 1681 he became the first European to reach the river's mouth. He claimed all the land of the Mississippi basin for France and named the new land Louisiana, in honor of the French king, Louis XIV.

Between 1797 and 1812, David Thompson explored the northwest and crossed the Rocky Mountains. He worked for an English trading company and was one of the first explorers to draw accurate maps.

In 1804 Meriwether Lewis and William Clark, Americans sent by President Thomas Jefferson, sailed up the Missouri River and rode over the Rocky Mountains, reaching the Pacific coast two years later.

KEY TO MAP

```
-----------   Hudson 1609
- - - - - -   Hudson 1610
~~~~~~~~~~~   Champlain
-·-·-·-·-·-   La Salle
············  Thompson
++++++++++++  Lewis & Clark
```

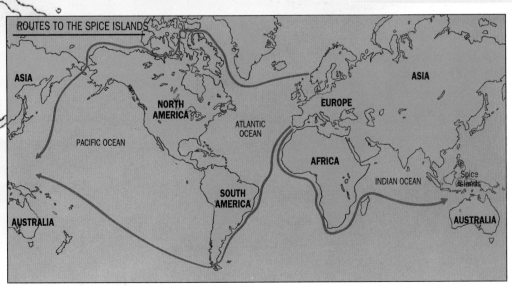

ROUTES TO THE SPICE ISLANDS

ASIA
NORTH AMERICA
PACIFIC OCEAN
ATLANTIC OCEAN
EUROPE
ASIA
AFRICA
INDIAN OCEAN
SOUTH AMERICA
Spice Islands
AUSTRALIA
AUSTRALIA

What they brought back

FURS AND BUFFALO SKINS

TOBACCO

POTATOES

PEOPLE

FEATHER AND BEAD WORK

PEOPLE OF NORTH AMERICA

During the early exploration of North America, most Native Americans were friendly to the Europeans. They believed there was enough land and food for all. The first settlers, the Pilgrims who sailed to America from England in 1620, were helped by Samoset and Squanto of the Masasoit tribe. They showed the Pilgrims how to plant corn and set fish traps.

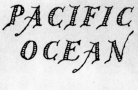

Pocahontas (right) was an Indian princess. Her father, Chief Powhatan, captured an Englishman, John Smith, who had killed two members of the Algonkin tribe. Powhatan threatened to kill Smith, but Pocahontas begged for his life and saved him.

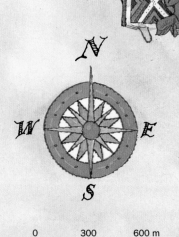

HORSES AND GUNS

Before the arrival of the Europeans, Native Americans did not have horses or guns. In battle they used bows, arrows, and tomahawks (axes made of stone). Horses and guns greatly changed the Native Americans' way of life. Horses were admired and respected by many tribes. Horses could carry much more than dogs and travel twice the distance in one day. This new mobility allowed these tribes to travel farther. Some tribes used horses to raid their neighbors and became great warriors. Others changed from a foraging to a hunting way of life. The tribes that hunted buffalo found they could follow the herds over vaster distances and hunt the animals more efficiently riding horses. The introduction of horses and guns had a significant and permanent impact on many Native American tribes.

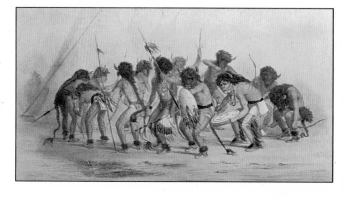

0   300   600 m

NATIVE AMERICANS

There were many different tribes living in North America. Each was a unique culture with its own laws, customs, and traditions. Here is a brief description of a few groups.

THE ARCTIC

The people who lived in the Arctic were hunters and fishers. They speared seals through holes made in the ice and made boats of seal skin called *kayaks*, which they used for fishing in the summer. In the winter they hunted polar bears in sleds pulled by husky dogs.

THE NORTHWEST COAST

The people of the northwest coast were expert fishers. They traveled in dugout canoes, which were often beautifully carved.

THE GREAT PLAINS

The people of the Plains followed the buffalo herds. When it was time for a hunt, the whole tribe set off together. Medicine men sang and danced to bring out the buffalo. The native people ate dried buffalo meat, and their tents, or *tipis*, were made of buffalo skin.

THE SOUTHWEST

The people of the southwest were farmers. They made beautiful pottery and baskets. Some tribes wove wonderful cloth. Some medicine men made pictures out of sand to help them work magic.

THE NORTHEAST

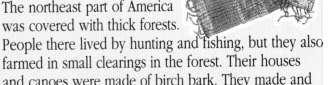

The northeast part of America was covered with thick forests. People there lived by hunting and fishing, but they also farmed in small clearings in the forest. Their houses and canoes were made of birch bark. They made and traded *wampum*—belts made of shells that they used as money.

35

EXPLORERS OF SOUTH AMERICA

The first European explorers of South America were the Spanish conquistadors, who were searching for gold. Until the 18th century, South America was practically unknown to explorers from other countries. Then, at last, the search for gold was replaced by a search for scientific knowledge. The new explorers wanted to find out about the animal and plant life. Their journeys took them deep into the rainforest, where they faced danger at every step: a thick rainforest hid poisonous snakes, jaguars, and unknown people, but the greatest danger to the Europeans was of catching an illness and fever.

ALEXANDER VON HUMBOLDT

This German explorer was rich enough to pay for his own expedition in 1799. He was eager to learn all he could about South America and traveled all over the continent, often at great risk. He explored the Orinoco River, climbed the high Andes Mountains, peered into the mouth of a live volcano, and got a shock from an electric eel. One of his discoveries was the Humboldt Current—a cold sea current off the coast of Peru.

Humboldt was interested in the peoples of South America. He saw that Europeans often treated them badly. When he returned home, he worked hard to tell others about this and to help bring about change.

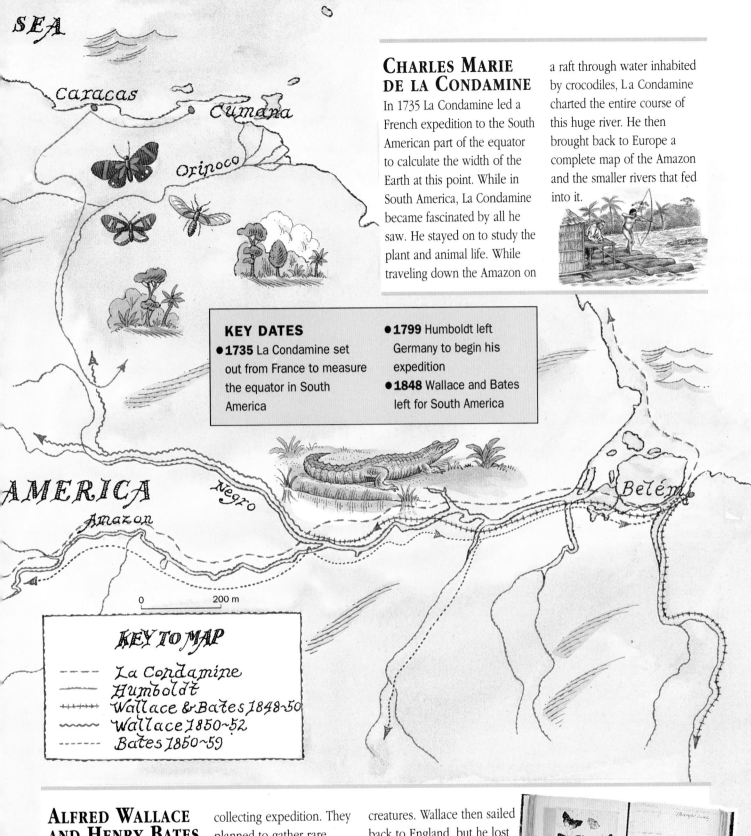

SEA

Caracas

Cumana

Orinoco

AMERICA

Amazon

Negro

Belém

0   200 m

CHARLES MARIE DE LA CONDAMINE

In 1735 La Condamine led a French expedition to the South American part of the equator to calculate the width of the Earth at this point. While in South America, La Condamine became fascinated by all he saw. He stayed on to study the plant and animal life. While traveling down the Amazon on a raft through water inhabited by crocodiles, La Condamine charted the entire course of this huge river. He then brought back to Europe a complete map of the Amazon and the smaller rivers that fed into it.

KEY DATES
- **1735** La Condamine set out from France to measure the equator in South America
- **1799** Humboldt left Germany to begin his expedition
- **1848** Wallace and Bates left for South America

KEY TO MAP
- - - - - La Condamine
———— Humboldt
+++++ Wallace & Bates 1848~50
~~~~~ Wallace 1850~52
- · - · - Bates 1850~59

ALFRED WALLACE AND HENRY BATES

These two friends from England were both enthusiastic naturalists (people who study animals and plants). In 1848 they set off for South America on a collecting expedition. They planned to gather rare specimens to sell in England in order, they hoped, to pay for the trip.

For three years they traveled together, studying unfamiliar plants and creatures. Wallace then sailed back to England, but he lost most of his collection when his ship caught fire. Bates stayed on in South America until 1859, writing about and sketching hundreds of new specimens.

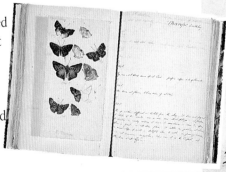

EXPLORING SOUTH AMERICA

The explorers who traveled down the Amazon were the first Europeans to enter the rainforests. For the most part, they journeyed by raft or canoe. It was an environment unlike anything they had ever seen.

Everywhere the explorers looked, there were strange, new things. The waters of the Amazon were full of life. There were alligators sixteen feet long, large swimming rodents called capybara, water snakes, and turtles. In some places there were piranha fish, which could strip a man's arm to the bone in ten minutes, and shoals of stingrays. Electric eels swam in the shallows.

Flocks of flamingoes and spoonbills flew overhead. In the trees were howler monkeys and parrots; sloths hung upside down from the branches. There was danger from jaguars and pumas. At night there were vampire bats that sucked the blood of many creatures. One of these bats bit Humboldt's pet dog.

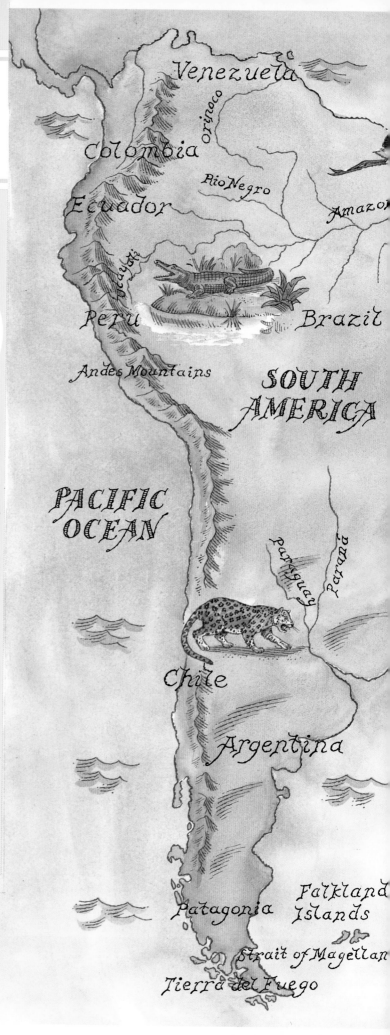

Venezuela
Orinoco
Colombia
Rio Negro
Ecuador
Amazon
Ucayali
Peru
Brazil
Andes Mountains
SOUTH AMERICA
PACIFIC OCEAN
Paraguay
Paraná
Chile
Argentina
Patagonia
Falkland Islands
Strait of Magellan
Tierra del Fuego

ATLANTIC OCEAN

0   300   600 m

What the explorers brought back

The explorers of South America brought back:

RUBBER

GOLD

PLATINUM

MAHOGANY

THE RUBBER TREE

The people of the rainforest showed Humboldt a tree which, when cut, oozed a sticky, milk-white sap. This was latex, the sap from which rubber is made.

THE PEOPLES OF SOUTH AMERICA

The explorers found many different groups of Native Americans living in the South American rainforest. They all lived primarily by farming, growing crops such as cassava, beans, corn, squash, and sweet potatoes. Cassava was their most important crop. Its roots contain poison, which the native people removed by grating and squeezing the roots. They ground the remains into meal for making bread.

The native people knew the rainforest very well. They knew all about the plants: which ones were poisonous and which could be used as food and medicine. They were skillful hunters, killing fish, animals, and birds of the rainforest for food. Their weapons included spears, bows and arrows, blowguns, nets, hooks, and potions for stunning fish.

The tribes of South America had customs, religions, and traditions that were very different from those Europeans were used to. Depending on the tribe, some people covered their bodies with painted designs and wore ornate jewelry. Others made holes in their cheeks with sharp pieces of bone or tattooed themselves all over. Children of the Arua tribe had their earlobes stretched by weights to appear more beautiful. One tribe, the Amazons, was led by women.

39

CAPTAIN COOK

Long after the other continents were explored, the Australian continent remained a mystery to Europeans. They believed there was a huge southern land, which they called "Terra Australis." They thought it was a magical place with unicorns and dragons where the rivers ran with jewels.

It took a long time to learn the truth because Australia is so far away from Europe. The Pacific Ocean is vast and it took months for a sailing ship to cross it. Taking enough food and water to last the voyage was also a problem. The exploration of the Pacific could only start when newer, faster sailing ships were developed.

ABEL TASMAN

In 1642 Abel Jansz Tasman, a Dutch captain, was sent to explore the South Pacific. He landed on a small island south of Australia and met fierce resistance from the native people. He claimed this island for Holland and named it Van Diemen's Land after the Governor General of the Dutch East Indies. Today we call it Tasmania after the Dutch sea captain.

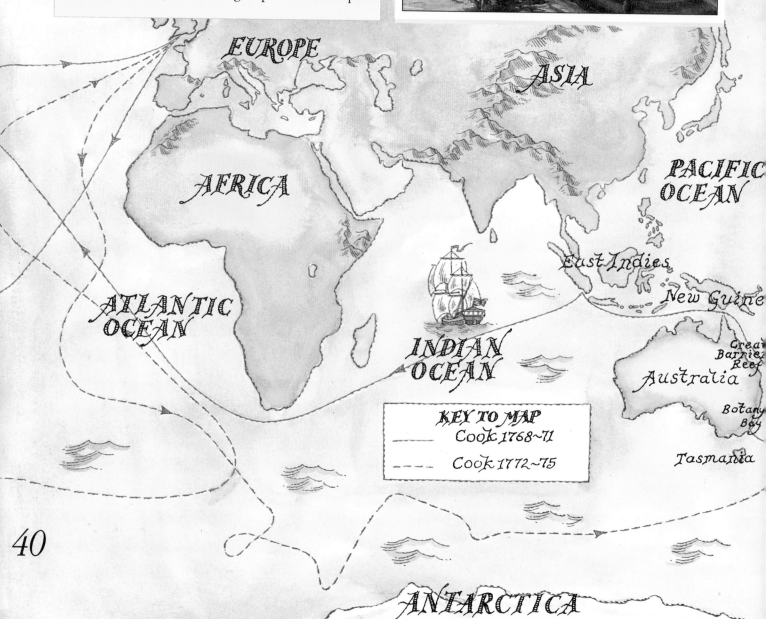

EUROPE

ASIA

PACIFIC OCEAN

AFRICA

East Indies

New Guinea

ATLANTIC OCEAN

INDIAN OCEAN

Great Barrier Reef

Australia

Botany Bay

Tasmania

KEY TO MAP
——— Cook 1768~71
- - - Cook 1772~75

ANTARCTICA

COOK'S FIRST AND SECOND JOURNEYS

James Cook was born in 1728, the son of a farm worker in Yorkshire, England. He joined the navy as an ordinary seaman, but rose quickly through the ranks, becoming captain of his first ship in 1767.

In 1768 he set out as leader of a scientific expedition to Tahiti in the Pacific Ocean, from where scientists planned to watch the planet Venus passing in front of the sun—a very rare event. After this, Cook had orders to explore the continent of Australia, which he knew lay somewhere in the South Pacific.

From Tahiti, Cook sailed in his ship, the *Endeavour*, all the way to New Zealand, carefully charting the coastline. He went on to Australia, landing first at Botany Bay and then sailing north towards the Great Barrier Reef, where his boat was shipwrecked. After making repairs, Cook

sailed back to England, arriving in 1771.

For his second voyage in 1772, Cook took two ships, the *Resolution* and the *Adventure*. On this journey he sailed further into the Pacific than any European had before him. The ships sailed close to the Antarctic Circle, meeting many

dangers such as icebergs, pack-ice, ferocious winds, and freezing fog. Cook also charted Tonga and Easter Island and discovered New Caledonia. On his journey home the explorer discovered the South Sandwich Islands and South Georgia in the Atlantic.

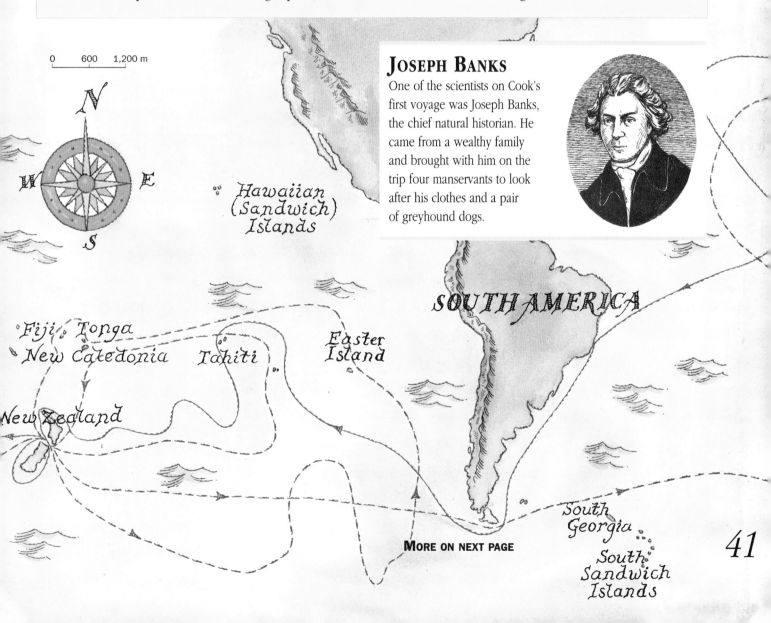

JOSEPH BANKS

One of the scientists on Cook's first voyage was Joseph Banks, the chief natural historian. He came from a wealthy family and brought with him on the trip four manservants to look after his clothes and a pair of greyhound dogs.

0   600   1,200 m

Hawaiian (Sandwich) Islands

SOUTH AMERICA

Fiji Tonga
New Caledonia   Tahiti   Easter Island

New Zealand

South Georgia

South Sandwich Islands

MORE ON NEXT PAGE

COOK'S FINAL VOYAGE

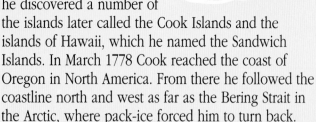

On his third voyage, Cook explored the Pacific Ocean to see how far north he could go. He took his two ships, the *Resolution* and the *Discovery*, and in 1776 sailed for the Pacific. There he discovered a number of the islands later called the Cook Islands and the islands of Hawaii, which he named the Sandwich Islands. In March 1778 Cook reached the coast of Oregon in North America. From there he followed the coastline north and west as far as the Bering Strait in the Arctic, where pack-ice forced him to turn back.

The two ships returned to spend the winter in Hawaii. The native people there believed Cook was a god. All went well until one of Cook's men died. The islanders knew then that the sailors were human like themselves. A little later, trouble broke out over the theft of one of Cook's boats and Cook was killed, clubbed to death by the men who had previously worshipped him.

COOK'S ACHIEVEMENTS

Cook cleared up the mystery of the area known as "Terra Australis." He was the first European to sail around Australia and map its coastline. He charted much of the Pacific Ocean and discovered several island groups.

On his second voyage, Cook took a ship's clock called a chronometer with him. For the first time on a round-the-world voyage, the clock kept going for the length of the journey. This allowed Cook to measure accurately the distance of the Earth from east to west (its longitude).

Cook was one of the first sea captains to find a solution to the disease scurvy. Every man in his crew was supplied with onions and ordered to eat them. He also gave the sailors pickled cabbage to eat and, when they refused, he ordered the officers to eat it to set an example. As a result, not one of Cook's men died from scurvy during these long voyages.

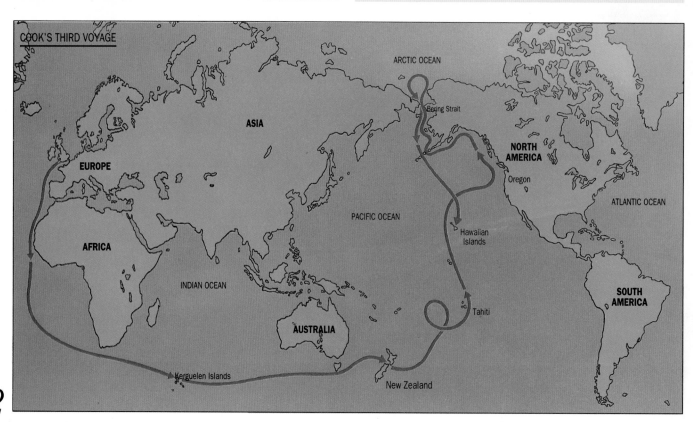

COOK'S THIRD VOYAGE

ARCTIC OCEAN

Bering Strait

ASIA

EUROPE

NORTH AMERICA

Oregon

ATLANTIC OCEAN

AFRICA

PACIFIC OCEAN

Hawaiian Islands

INDIAN OCEAN

AUSTRALIA

Tahiti

SOUTH AMERICA

Kerguelen Islands

New Zealand

ARCTIC OCEAN

Siberia

Alaska

Bering Strait

Aleutian Islands

0 300 600 1,200 m

N
W   E
S

PACIFIC OCEAN

Hawaiian (Sandwich) Islands

Canada

NORTH AMERICA

Vancouver Island

Oregon

United States of America

THE NATIVE PEOPLES

Cook and his crew became friendly with the South Pacific islanders, who rowed out to meet them. The Maoris of New Zealand, however, attacked the Europeans when the travelers tried to land. During the second voyage, ten crew members were killed by Maoris.

THE POLYNESIANS

The islanders Cook met had made their own journey thousands of years before to spread through the Pacific. They had set out in large dug-out canoes to settle the empty islands scattered across this vast ocean. They took seeds and young trees, pigs, dogs, and chickens with them. Coconuts and yams, bananas and breadfruit were also all carried across the sea by the Polynesians.

Scholars think these people used the sun and stars to help them find their way. They must have known a great deal about the tides and winds of the Pacific.

43

EXPLORERS OF AUSTRALIA

Captain Cook was English, so the British claimed Australia as their possession. By the late 1790s, Britain was using Australia as a place to send prisoners. The prisoners never returned to England.

In the early days, the prisoners and their guards stayed in Botany Bay. The mountains behind the bay made it difficult for people to travel far inland. But as the colony became more and more populated, new land was needed.

Gregory Blaxland, William Wentworth, and William Lawson were the first Europeans to cross the mountains in 1813. They were looking for new land for their animals. They found that good land lay beyond the mountains. Soon other settlers followed their lead and spread inland from Botany Bay.

The land was watered by rivers. The settlers believed there had to be a great sea or lake somewhere in the center of Australia. In 1828 Charles Sturt took a rowboat up the Macquarie River to look for it. He rowed 2,000 miles and faced swamps and drought, hostile tribes, and deadly snakes. He did not find a great sea, but he did discover the Darling River.

In 1844 Sturt set out from Adelaide to trace the Murray River. The men crossed a desert so hot and dry that they had to dig shelters against the sun. The journey lasted 17 months and began to open up the middle of Australia to the European settlers.

INDIAN OCEAN

Darwin

N

W E

S

Great Sandy Desert

KEY TO MAP
- - - - Blaxland, Wentworth & Lawson
··········· Sturt 1828~29
———— Sturt 1844
- · - · - Burke
~~~~~ Stuart

Great Victoria Desert

0   100   200 m

Perth

PEOPLE OF THE BUSH

The bush is the name given to the sparse, uncultivated countryside of Australia. For the Europeans, it was a very dangerous place. But the Aborigines, the people who lived in the bush, knew it well and could find food and water even in the hottest and driest parts. They knew where to look for wild figs and bush tomatoes, honey ants and grubs. The men fished and hunted kangaroo. The women and children gathered berries.

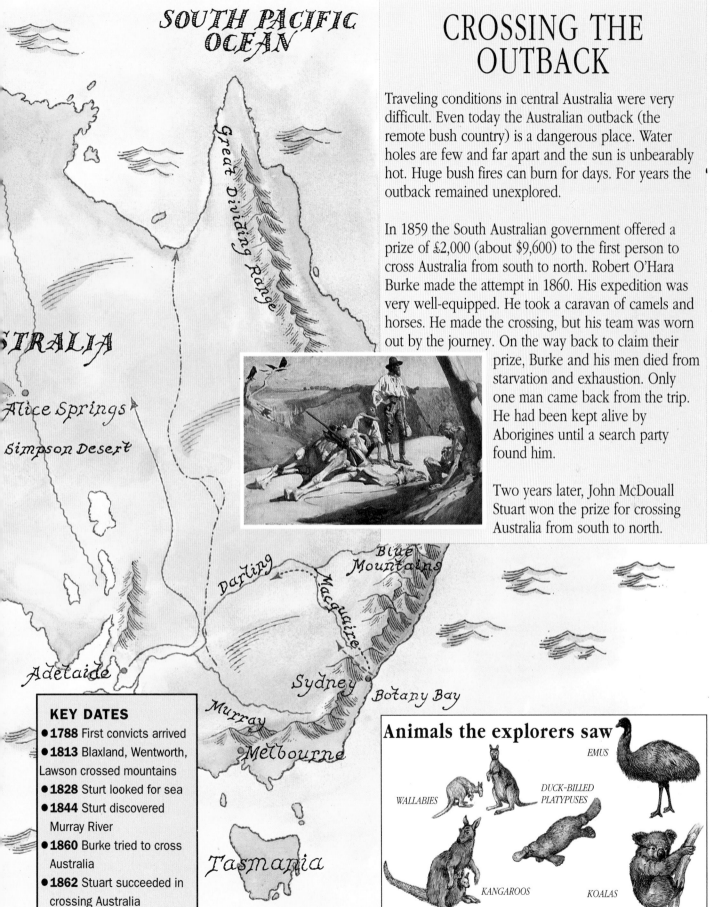

SOUTH PACIFIC OCEAN

Great Dividing Range

*TRALIA

Alice Springs

Simpson Desert

Blue Mountains

Darling

Macquarie

Adelaide

Sydney

Botany Bay

Murray

Melbourne

Tasmania

CROSSING THE OUTBACK

Traveling conditions in central Australia were very difficult. Even today the Australian outback (the remote bush country) is a dangerous place. Water holes are few and far apart and the sun is unbearably hot. Huge bush fires can burn for days. For years the outback remained unexplored.

In 1859 the South Australian government offered a prize of £2,000 (about $9,600) to the first person to cross Australia from south to north. Robert O'Hara Burke made the attempt in 1860. His expedition was very well-equipped. He took a caravan of camels and horses. He made the crossing, but his team was worn out by the journey. On the way back to claim their prize, Burke and his men died from starvation and exhaustion. Only one man came back from the trip. He had been kept alive by Aborigines until a search party found him.

Two years later, John McDouall Stuart won the prize for crossing Australia from south to north.

KEY DATES
- **1788** First convicts arrived
- **1813** Blaxland, Wentworth, Lawson crossed mountains
- **1828** Sturt looked for sea
- **1844** Sturt discovered Murray River
- **1860** Burke tried to cross Australia
- **1862** Stuart succeeded in crossing Australia

Animals the explorers saw

EMUS

DUCK-BILLED PLATYPUSES

WALLABIES

KANGAROOS

KOALAS

45

EXPLORERS OF AFRICA

Long before the Europeans entered Africa, the Arabs were trading there. The continent was criss-crossed with trade routes used by the Arab merchants. They brought salt and gold with them, which they traded for ivory and slaves. They carried the goods in camel caravans. Sometimes as many as 1,000 camels made the journey. These caravans crossed deserts and high mountains, traveling vast distances to reach the great markets of Africa.

The first Europeans to settle in Africa were the Dutch. They settled in the Cape of Good Hope in 1652. Gradually they spread further north and, in 1760, an elephant hunter named Jacob Coetsee crossed the Orange River. Once they had crossed this natural barrier, the Europeans began to spread out across South Africa.

At first, Europeans went to Africa to trade, especially in slaves. Then they went as hunters, many of them killing elephants for their ivory. Later came missionaries who wanted to convert the Africans to Christianity. Some missionaries also tried to end the slave trade.

The map shows: Tangier, Atlas Mountains, Sahara Desert, Hogga Mountains, Timbuktu, Falémé, Jenne (Djenné), Hausa Country, Niger, ATLANTIC OCEAN

RENE-AUGUSTE CAILLIÉ

On the southern edge of the Sahara Desert in North Africa is the city of Timbuktu. This was one of the most important trading centers of Africa. To the Europeans it was known as "the forbidden city" because the Muslims there did not allow Christians to enter. The French Geographical Society offered a prize to the first Christian to get into Timbuktu. A young Frenchman, René-Auguste Caillié, decided to try. He learned to speak Arabic and he studied the Muslim Holy Book, the *Koran.*

In March 1827 Caillié disguised himself as a Muslim and traveled to the west coast of Africa.

There he joined a salt caravan on its way to Timbuktu. After two months on the road, he collapsed, sick with malaria and scurvy. The old woman who looked after him guessed he was not a Muslim, but she kept his secret. In March 1828, an entire year after setting out, the caravan reached Djenné, where it boarded a boat for Timbuktu.

It was another 500 miles before Caillié got his first glimpse of Timbuktu. He entered the city, but by now he was in danger as his disguise was beginning to arouse suspicion. He managed to escape over the Atlas Mountains and get back to France to claim his prize.

Cairo

Nile

AFRICA

Zaire (Congo)

THE AFRICAN SOCIETY

In 1788 a group of rich British formed the African Society. Its aim was to explore Africa. The society hired a young Scottish doctor, Mungo Park, to make the first expedition.

In 1795 Park took with him two interpreters and some presents for trading. He endured many hardships including suffering from extreme hunger and thirst and being taken prisoner by Moors, Muslims of North Africa. When Park returned to Scotland, he wrote a book about his travels. Before long he became very famous.

In May 1805 Park began his second expedition. He planned to travel down the Niger River to the sea, which would have made him the first European to do so. He started down the Falémé River with 44 men, but by August, when he reached the Niger, only ten men were still alive–disease had killed the rest. By November, there were only five men left. That was the last that was heard of Mungo Park. He never reached the mouth of the Niger.

Five years later, a Mandingo, West African, guide went to find out what had happened. He learned that Park and his men had crossed into the Hausa city-state. The boat they were in was wrecked by rapids and they were attacked by tribesmen. The Europeans did not survive the fierce river currents or the attack.

N

W   E

S

Zambezi

KEY TO MAP
~~~~~~ *Park 1795~96*
------ *Park 1805~6*
.... *Caillié*

0   300   600 m

Orange

INDIAN OCEAN

Cape of Good Hope

Animals the explorers saw

The Europeans saw animals they had never seen before such as:

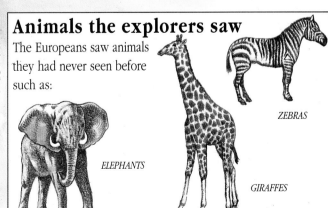

ZEBRAS

ELEPHANTS

GIRAFFES

MORE ON NEXT PAGE

47

BURTON AND SPEKE

In the far northern part of Africa, the mighty Nile River spreads out into the Mediterranean Sea. The oldest maps plot its route through Egypt, but until the middle of the 19th century, its source (the place where the river begins) was a mystery. Ivory traders told of a great lake in the center

of Africa, filled by the melting snow from a high range of mountains. When European explorers tried to trace the river back to the mountains, waterfalls and rapids blocked their way.

In 1856 Britain's Royal Geographical Society raised £1,000 (about $5,000) to pay for an expedition to search for the source of the Nile. As leaders, they chose Richard Burton and John Speke, both army officers. The society instructed the men to look for the great lake by traveling inland from the island of Zanzibar on Africa's east coast, then to go north to the mountains in search of the source of the Nile.

TRAVELING BY LAND

Burton and Speke took so much luggage with them on their journeys that they needed 130 porters and 30 donkeys to carry it all. Nevertheless, they lost much of it as they crossed dangerous rivers and swamps. When both men became ill, the porters had to carry them, as well as their belongings.

Hoggar Mountains

Sahara Desert

AFRICA

0   100   200 m

KEY TO MAP
----- Burton & Speke
——— Speke

AFRICAN DISEASES

In the 19th century, Europeans found the African climate so unhealthy to them that they nicknamed the continent "the white man's grave." The medicine brought by Burton and Speke was no protection against malaria and fever. Burton's legs became paralyzed and useless. A small beetle crawled into Speke's ear, causing a horrible infection. For a time he was blind, and he could not see Lake Tanganyika when the expedition reached it.

Za

N
W   E
S

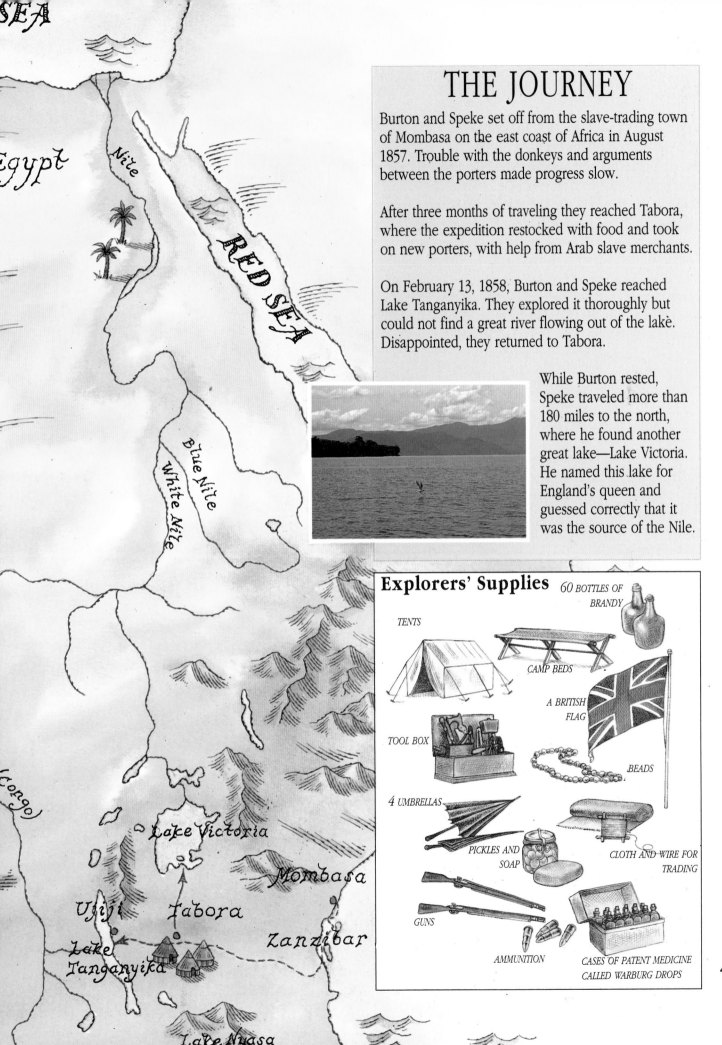

THE JOURNEY

Burton and Speke set off from the slave-trading town of Mombasa on the east coast of Africa in August 1857. Trouble with the donkeys and arguments between the porters made progress slow.

After three months of traveling they reached Tabora, where the expedition restocked with food and took on new porters, with help from Arab slave merchants.

On February 13, 1858, Burton and Speke reached Lake Tanganyika. They explored it thoroughly but could not find a great river flowing out of the lake. Disappointed, they returned to Tabora.

While Burton rested, Speke traveled more than 180 miles to the north, where he found another great lake—Lake Victoria. He named this lake for England's queen and guessed correctly that it was the source of the Nile.

Explorers' Supplies

60 BOTTLES OF BRANDY

TENTS

CAMP BEDS

A BRITISH FLAG

TOOL BOX

BEADS

4 UMBRELLAS

PICKLES AND SOAP

CLOTH AND WIRE FOR TRADING

GUNS

AMMUNITION

CASES OF PATENT MEDICINE CALLED WARBURG DROPS

SEA

Egypt

Nile

RED SEA

Blue Nile

White Nile

(Congo)

Lake Victoria

Mombasa

Tabora

Ujiji

Zanzibar

Lake Tanganyika

Lake Nyasa

49

LIVINGSTONE AND STANLEY

David Livingstone, the most famous European explorer of Africa, was missing. In 1866 he had left Britain to look for the source of the Nile River. Five years later, nothing had been heard of him. An American newspaper, the *New York Herald,* sent out its best reporter, Henry Stanley, with the command, "Find Livingstone!"

Stanley took a huge caravan of pack animals and porters with him. He marched for eight months through deserts and swamps until he came to the town of Ujiji near Lake Tanganyika. There he found David Livingstone, tired, ill, and dressed in rags. Taking off his hat, Stanley said the now-famous words, "Dr. Livingstone, I presume?" He had traveled halfway across Africa to find the man he was looking for.

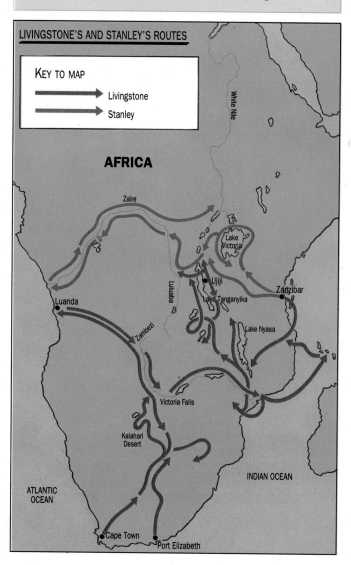

LIVINGSTONE'S AND STANLEY'S ROUTES

KEY TO MAP
→ Livingstone
→ Stanley

AFRICA

White Nile

Zaïre

Lake Victoria

Luluaba

Ujiji

Lake Tanganyika

Zanzibar

Luanda

Zambezi

Lake Nyasa

Victoria Falls

Kalahari Desert

INDIAN OCEAN

ATLANTIC OCEAN

Cape Town

Port Elizabeth

DAVID LIVINGSTONE

Born in Scotland in 1813 to a poor family, David Livingstone was interested in natural history as a boy. Later he studied medicine, then became a minister with the London Missionary Society.

Livingstone first went to Africa in 1840 to teach the people who lived there about Christianity. He wanted to open up more routes to the interior of Africa so that other missionaries could reach the local people. He crossed southern Africa from west to east (the first European to do so) and sailed down the Zambezi River. He crossed the Kalahari Desert, where the ground was so dry his party had to dig down nine feet before they found water.

He was the first European to see Victoria Falls, which the Africans called the "Smoke that Thunders," and to discover Lake Nyasa. He spent half of his life exploring. In 1873, exhausted and ill, he died on the shores of Lake Tanganyika.

HENRY MORTON STANLEY

Born in 1841, Stanley spent his childhood in a workhouse in Wales. He ran away to sea and made his home in the United States. Later he got a job writing for the *New York Herald* newspaper. After his meeting with Livingstone, he continued exploring and sailed down the Zaïre River deep into Africa. He emerged on the west coast after 999 days in the interior. His boat, the *Lady Alice,* was made in sections so that it could be taken apart and carried across or around dangerous parts of the river.

Explorers' Supplies

Livingstone took only a few things on his journey across Africa. These were:

4 GUNS TO SHOOT GAME TO FEED HIS PARTY

BEADS FOR TRADING

A SMALL TENT

SPARE CLOTHES

His most precious possessions were:

HIS DIARY

A MEDICINE CHEST

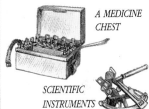

SCIENTIFIC INSTRUMENTS

Stanley took far more with him. The porters carrying his possessions were arranged by size and age:

SHORT ONES CARRIED SACKS OF BEADS

TALL ONES CARRIED BALES OF CLOTH

THE OLDEST AND MOST TRUSTWORTHY CARRIED THE SCIENTIFIC INSTRUMENTS

LIVINGSTONE AND THE AFRICANS

Livingstone spent much of his life fighting against slavery. He was much loved by the African people he met because he did all he could to help them. He always carried a medicine chest and used his skills as a doctor to heal sick people whom he met on his travels.

He had two African servants, Susi and Chuma, who went everywhere with him. These two men stayed with the doctor until he died. Then they carried his body, which they had preserved with salt, for hundreds of miles through swamp and forest, back to Zanzibar on the coast, so that he could be buried in his own country. His heart, though, they buried in Africa.

EXPLORERS OF THE NORTH POLE

ROBERT PEARY

In 1909 two men took part in a race to reach the North Pole. Robert Peary and Dr. Frederick Cook were both Americans. Peary planned his expedition very carefully. He took 133 dogs and 12 sleds and used Inuit (Eskimo) guides. On April 6,1909, Peary reached the North Pole with his servant and African-American friend, Matthew Henson, and four Inuit. Dr. Cook later claimed he had reached the Pole before Peary, but people now believe that Cook was mistaken.

At the top of the world lies the coldest ocean on

Earth. It is the Arctic Ocean, where the water freezes into solid ice that can trap a ship forever.

For thousands of years people have known about the Arctic Ocean and its dangers. The ancient Greeks had explored this area and they believed it marked the end of the Earth.

Europeans began to explore it a few years after Columbus, da Gama, and Magellan made their great journeys of discovery. The captains of these European expeditions were looking for a northern passage to the Spice Islands. Spain and Portugal had claimed the two best routes by going south. Other nations hoped to find a different way by going far north.

FRIDTJOF NANSEN

Nansen was a Norwegian, born in 1861. He knew that the waters of the Arctic, though frozen, moved very slowly. He believed that if he built a boat strong enough to withstand the ice, he could drift in it towards the North Pole. The attempt took three years. Although Nansen didn't reach the Pole, his journey taught other explorers a great deal about living in the Arctic.

KEY TO MAP

——— Barents
- - - - Bering
·-·-· Nansen
——— Peary

laska

Bering Strait

Siberia

OCEAN

Arctic Circle

ASIA

KEY DATES
- **1596** Barents wintered in the Arctic
- **1724** Bering left for eastern Asia
- **1893-6** Nansen sailed across the Arctic
- **1909** Peary reached the North Pole

VITUS BERING

Bering served in the Russian Navy. In 1724 Peter the Great sent him to find out whether Asia was joined to North America. Bering discovered that the two continents were separated by a strait (narrow channel). This body of water is now named the Bering Strait.

WILLEM BARENTS

The Dutch sent Willem Barents to explore the areas to the north and east of Norway, where they believed they might find a northeast passage to the Pacific Ocean.

In 1596 Barents was sailing off the coast of Novaya Zemlya in the Arctic Ocean when the sea began to freeze. Winter was beginning and the crew was trapped.

Ice formed around the ship, cracking its timbers and forcing it up out of the water. The sailors walked across the ice until they got to shore, carrying wood from the ship with them. They built a hut out of the wood and they stayed there all through the winter, on a shore that they named "Ice Haven." It was so cold that the wine froze in their glasses and the sheets froze on their beds. The men survived the winter by hunting animals and living off the supplies from the ship.

In 1871, nearly 300 years later, another expedition found the hut, just as Barents and his men had left it. The cooking pots and weapons, the ship's clock, and even the cabin boy's boots, were still there, preserved by the cold.

PEOPLE OF THE ARCTIC

The Inuit were expert at surviving in the extreme cold. Their clothes were warmer and lighter than anything the explorers could make. They dressed in jackets and pants of sealskin. Their boots were stuffed with moss. In winter they traveled by dogsled and, when the thaw came, they used kayaks— canoes made of whale bone and hide.

53

EXPLORERS OF THE SOUTH POLE

The explorers who tried to reach the South Pole faced terrible dangers. Ships sailing around Antarctica met icebergs big enough to sink them. To the south, the Ross Ice Shelf, a vast cliff of ice, bars the way to the Antarctic continent. The land at the South Pole is a mixture of snow-fields and mountain peaks. Hidden under the snow there are crevasses—deep cracks in the ice that can swallow up a sled or a team of dogs. Hunger, fatigue, cold, and frostbite are all enemies of travelers in the Antarctic.

TWO POLES

There are two South Poles. One is the South Magnetic Pole. This is the point that draws the needle of the compass. The other is the geographic South Pole. This is in the exact center of the Arctic Circle and is the point that Scott and Amundsen were trying to reach. There are two North Poles also.

JAMES CLARK ROSS

An officer in the British navy, James Clark Ross was the first man to discover the North Magnetic Pole between 1829 and 1833.

He also explored Antarctica. In 1841 he took two strong ships, the *Erebus* and the *Terror*, south through pack-ice and past live volcanoes until they came to a great wall of ice. This is now called the Ross Ice Shelf.

SOUTH AMERICA

ATLANTIC OCEAN

Weddell Sea

Ronne Ice Shelf

ANTARCTICA

South Pole

Ross Sea

Bay of Whales

Ross Ice Shelf

McMurdo Sound

South Magnetic Pole

PACIFIC OCEAN

Antarctic Circle

RACE FOR THE SOUTH POLE

In 1911 two expeditions set out to reach the South Pole. One was British: Captain Robert Scott sailed from London towards Antarctica in the *Terra Nova*. He took a large team of scientists with him, including a film cameraman. When he reached Melbourne, Australia, Scott found a telegram waiting for him. It was from Roald Amundsen, a Norwegian explorer, who planned to race him to the Pole. Amundsen's team started the journey from his base in the Bay of Whales on October 20, 1911. They traveled quickly because they had little to carry. On December 14, 1911, they reached the South Pole, where they raised the Norwegian flag and put up a tent. Inside, they left letters for Scott. Then they returned to their ship and sailed safely home.

Scott left from his base at McMurdo Sound on November 1, 1911, but the ponies that he planned to use in the final stretch to the Pole died in the extreme cold. Scott's men had to help pull the sleds themselves because Scott had not brought enough dogs. The expedition soon ran into more trouble. The men grew very tired and Scott had to send back the sleds one after another, until there was only one left. On January 18, 1912, Scott and four teammates reached the South Pole. There they found the Norwegian flag, so they knew that Amundsen had beaten them to it. They started to make their way back to base, but they were tired and suffering badly from frostbite. Not one of them reached the base camp. All five men died on the way.

What the explorers took

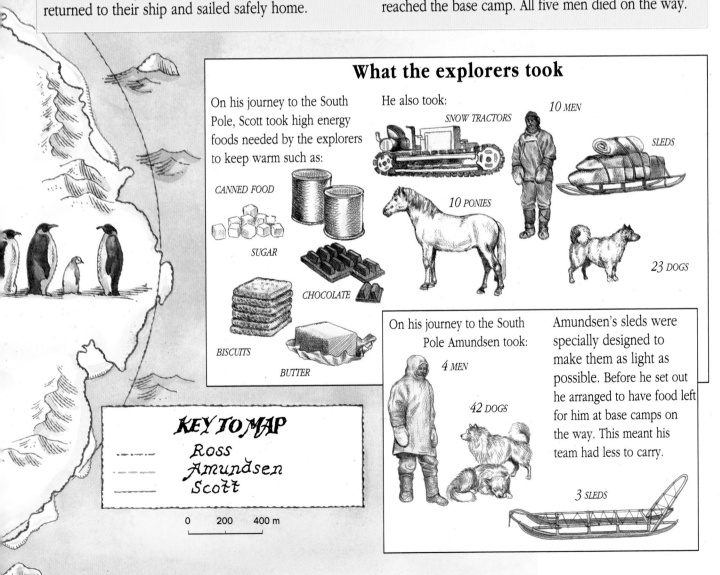

On his journey to the South Pole, Scott took high energy foods needed by the explorers to keep warm such as:

CANNED FOOD

SUGAR

CHOCOLATE

BISCUITS

BUTTER

He also took:

SNOW TRACTORS

10 MEN

SLEDS

10 PONIES

23 DOGS

On his journey to the South Pole Amundsen took:

4 MEN

42 DOGS

3 SLEDS

Amundsen's sleds were specially designed to make them as light as possible. Before he set out he arranged to have food left for him at base camps on the way. This meant his team had less to carry.

KEY TO MAP

------ Ross
– – – Amundsen
——— Scott

0   200   400 m

55

OCEAN EXPLORATION

Deep down at the bottom of the ocean it is pitch dark and very cold. The pressure of the water becomes more and more intense the further down you go. People have only been able to explore the great depths of the oceans within the last 150 years or so as a result of technological advances.

The first undersea explorers were skin divers who hunted for pearls, sponges, and coral. They could only stay down for as long as they could hold their breath. Then, about 400 years ago, people began to look for ways to go deeper and stay down longer. In 1624 Cornelius Drebbel, a Dutchman, built the first successful submarine. It was egg-shaped and made of wood. Twelve oarsmen rowed it along.

THE DIVING SUIT

In 1829 a German, Augustus Siebe, designed the diving-suit. The boots were made of brass or lead and were very heavy in order to stop the diver from floating up to the surface.

THE DIVING BELL

Another idea developed in the 16th century was the diving bell. This was a metal waterproof container filled with air. The diver went into it and was lowered to the bottom of the sea, where he stayed until the air in the bell was used up.

In the early 18th century, Edmund Halley invented a way of changing the air supply inside the bell by lowering barrels of fresh air down to it.

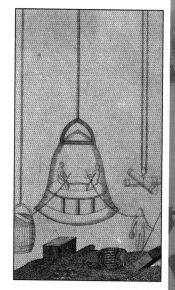

HMS CHALLENGER

The first ship equipped for ocean exploration, HMS *Challenger*, set out from England in 1872 to explore and measure the Pacific, Atlantic, and Indian oceans. The scientists found that the sea bed has mountains, valleys, and even underwater volcanoes, and that life exists deep below the ocean's surface. They measured the deepest sea in the world, the Mariana Trench in the Pacific, where the ocean floor is more than 36,000 feet deep.

THE BATHYSPHERE AND BATHYSCAPHE

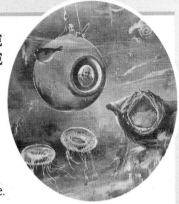

In 1930 Otis Barton and William Beebe invented the bathysphere, a steel ball with quartz portholes. Using this vessel the men reached a depth of about 3,000 feet, the deepest that anyone had gone.

The bathyscaphe, or "deep boat," was invented by Auguste Piccard. In 1960 it touched an incredible depth of over 35,800 feet. Piccard's son, Jacques, and Don Walsh, the two men inside, found that creatures and plants lived even at this depth.

THE AQUALUNG

The aqualung was invented in 1943 by the French underwater explorer, Jacques-Yves Cousteau, and by an engineer, Emile Gagnan. It allowed divers to swim to depths of almost 100 feet without being attached to a ship. This is because they carried their own air supply with them in a cylinder fastened to their back. A tube took the air from the cylinder to the diver's mouth.

THE DANGERS OF OCEAN EXPLORATION

Deep-sea diving has long been dangerous because of a condition known as "the bends," which can cripple or kill a diver. This happens when a diver comes up to the surface too quickly, so that bubbles of nitrogen form in the blood. Although we know how to prevent it, divers are still at risk from the bends as well as from problems brought about by heat loss and from "rapture of the deep"—a condition sometimes caused by breathing nitrogen under pressure. This causes a type of drunkenness.

One way of avoiding these problems is to use robots. They can be sent down to gather samples and take photographs. They are also used to repair oil pipelines. Another way is to build a saturation habitat (an underwater station) for the divers. These have been constructed underwater at depths of up to almost 600 feet. They are crewed by divers living there for days or weeks at a time.

SPACE EXPLORATION

Throughout history people have been fascinated by the mystery of what lies beyond our planet. Limited to watching and calculating from Earth, we have been unable, until the second half of the 20th century, to explore the vast unknown expanses of space.

Born in 1473, the Polish astronomer Copernicus (left) was the first person to explain that the planets move around the sun. Galileo, an Italian born in 1564, invented a telescope used to discover Jupiter's satellites and the craters on the moon.

As telescopes became more sophisticated, astronomers discovered more about different planets and solar systems. Pluto, at the furthest edge of our solar system, was named in 1930. Astronomers saw huge dying stars called supernovas, which shone very brightly, then disappeared. However, telescopes showed astronomers only a limited amount. To learn more about space, they needed to travel in space. A German, Wernher von Braun, designed the first working rocket, the *V-2*, which was used by the Germans in World War II. After the war, von Braun helped the Americans build space rockets. The first American rockets reached a height of 70 miles.

PEOPLE IN SPACE

In 1957 the Soviet Union launched the first manufactured satellite to orbit the Earth. It

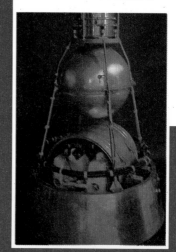

was called *Sputnik*. They later sent up another satellite, containing a dog: Laika. In 1961 the Russians sent the first person into space: Yuri Gagarin. He orbited the Earth once and landed 108 minutes later. In 1983 American Sally Ride became the first woman to travel in space.

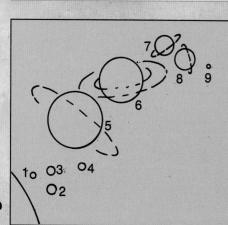

Mean distance of planets from the sun	
1 Mercury:	35,980,000 m
2 Venus:	67,240,000 m
3 Earth:	92,960,000 m
4 Mars:	141,640,000 m
5 Jupiter:	483,720,000 m
6 Saturn:	890,600,000 m
7 Uranus:	1,777,020,000 m
8 Neptune:	2,799,440,000 m
9 Pluto:	3,654,410,000 m

. . . AND ON THE MOON

By the early 1960s, it was a race between the United States and the Soviet Union to put the first person on the moon. The Americans were first in 1969. All over the world, millions watched on television as Neil Armstrong and Buzz Aldrin stepped out of the *Apollo 11* space capsule onto the moon's surface. Armstrong called it "one small step for man, a giant leap for mankind."

On subsequent trips, astronauts have brought back rock samples. Scientists studying them have learned much about the moon's age and make-up.

BEYOND THE MOON

In 1977 the United States sent out two probes to explore the solar system and beyond: *Voyager 1* and *Voyager 2* both headed for Jupiter. *Voyager 1* then left the solar system and is now traveling in outer space. *Voyager 2* was programmed to travel past Saturn, Uranus, and Neptune, taking pictures as it went. The distance between the outer planets is enormous. It took *Voyager 2* five years to travel from Saturn to Uranus and another three years to travel to Neptune. The pictures taken by *Voyager 2* from millions of miles away show us things which no living person has ever seen before: Jupiter's red storm spot, Saturn's ice rings, and volcanoes on one of the moons that circles Neptune.

If people are ever to reach these distant planets of our solar system, they will have to remain in space for a very long time. In 1986 the Russians set up a space station, Mir, where astronauts live and work for several months as part of an experiment to find out how long people can stay safely in space. Another space station is being developed by NASA (National Aeronautics and Space Administration) for use in the mid 1990s. After that, NASA will attempt a landing on the planet Mars as the next great step in the story of space exploration.

59

THE FUTURE OF EXPLORATION

We have now explored almost all of the Earth's land surface. Because of this, modern-day exploration is quite different from what it was in previous centuries. Gone are the days when courageous men and women set out for unexplored territories, not knowing whether they would survive the hazards of unknown peoples, strange diseases, or wild animals. Modern explorers still have uncharted territories on Earth to explore such as the densest parts of the rainforest, the Antarctic regions, and the oceans. Most explorers of the 20th century are scientists and conservationists, eager to learn about the Earth and its climate, the balance that exists between all of the Earth's living things and ways to preserve and protect this balance.

THE ANTARCTIC

Antarctica was the last land surface on Earth to be fully explored when, in 1958, an expedition crossed the continent for the first time. Large areas of this freezing continent are still not known to us in any detail, but this is gradually changing since many international scientific stations are now based there. Scientists study the layers of ice, which show the composition of the snow that has fallen over the last 160,000 years. From this they can find out about long-term changes in Earth's climate and atmosphere.

THE RAINFORESTS

The tropical rainforests of Africa and South America contain millions of different animal and plant species, most of which have not been identified or named. In the more remote areas, there is still a lot of scientific exploration that can be done, especially with regard to the "canopy" of the rainforest (this is the name given to the mass of foliage high up in the trees).

Exploration has damaged the rainforests. It has led to people living outside the area destroying the rainforest for their own profit by lumbering, mining, and cattle-grazing. Only now are scientists going there to study the plants and animals of the rainforest in an effort to reverse the damage that has been caused.

STILL UNEXPLORED

Other areas of the Earth that have been only partly explored include high mountain areas, underground rivers and caves (left), the ocean bed, and desert areas. Projects continue to bring to light new facts on the Earth's make-up and to monitor the changes that are taking place, such as the expansion of the desert regions.

THE SKY IS THE LIMIT

As long as there have been places to explore, there have been people willing to take the risks and challenges involved in exploration. The greatest challenge in the 21st century for these men and women will be the continued exploration of space. Space travel has advanced in leaps and bounds, and it is possible that in the future someone will step on to the planet Mars. The wonder and vastness of space beckons to all those who consider themselves explorers.

INDEX

ACKNOWLEDGEMENTS

Senior designer: Susi Martin
Designers: Jane Warring, Brazzle Atkins
Editor: Sarah Allen
Picture Researchers: Lorraine Sennett, Liz Heasman
American text changes: Iris Rosoff

Illustrators: John Woodcock (Spectron Artists): main maps; Tony Lodge (Spectron Artists): inset maps; Kevin Jones Associates: pp22-23, pp56-57 & pp58-59; Lindi Norton: pp4-5; Bob Venables (Spectron Artists): all other artwork.

Photographs: Ancient Art & Architecture: 29; Bibliothèque Nationale: 12-13, 15; Bodleian Library, MS.Bodl.264, fol.259v: 16; Bridgeman Art Library: 3, 27, 34, 35, 53; Bruce Coleman: 2, 38; Dagli Orti: 18, 19, 20, 24, 28; Mary Evans Picture Library: 3, 9, 11, 12, 16, 20, 22, 34, 40, 44, 45, 46, 48, 51, 52, 54, 56, 57; Michael Holford: 6, 7; Chris Howes: 61; Hulton Deutsch Collection: 30; David Keith Jones/Images of Africa Photobank: 49; Mansell Collection: 24; Natural History Museum: 3, 37; National Maritime Museum: 41; Royal Geographical Society: 33, 61; Royal Geographical Society, London/Bridgeman Art Library: 8, 36, 38, 43, 48; Science Photo Library: 58, 59, 60, 61; Werner Forman Archive: 3.

First published in 1993 by HarperCollins Children's Books, an imprint of: HarperCollins Publishers Ltd, 77-85 Fulham Palace Road, London W6 8JB

Every effort has been made to contact the holders of copyright material, but if any have been inadvertently overlooked, the publishers will be pleased to make any necessary amendments.